DATE			

The
Father-Daughter
Dance

Insight, Inspiration, and Understanding for
Every Woman and Her Father

Barbara Goulter
and
Joan Minninger, Ph.D.

G. P. PUTNAM'S SONS
New York

Permissions appear on pages 243–44

G. P. Putnam's Sons
Publishers Since 1838
200 Madison Avenue
New York, NY 10016

Library of Congress Cataloging-in-Publication Data

Goulter, Barbara.
The father-daughter dance : insight, inspiration, and understanding for every
woman and her father / Barbara Goulter and Joan Minninger.
p.   cm.
ISBN 0-399-13826-9 (alk. paper)
1.   Fathers and daughters.   I. Minninger, Joan.   II. Title.
HQ755.85.G68   1993
306.874′2—dc20   92-32668 CIP

Designed by Rhea Braunstein

Printed in the United States of America
1   2   3   4   5   6   7   8   9   10

This book is printed on acid-free paper.
∞

In remembrance of my father and Neil Goulter
And with today's love to my mother and to Vic
—B.G.

In Memoriam, Bob Goulding
To Kyra
—J.M.

CONTENTS

ACKNOWLEDGMENTS

To the late Robert L. Goulding, M.D., and to Mary McClure Goulding, M.S.W., brilliant architects of Redecision Therapy, who taught me how to help fathers and daughters move through their psychological impasses; and to Lillian K. Cartwright, who has impressed me with the theory of intermittent reinforcement and other wonders of the interior world.

To my editor John Dutt; I have been blessed to work with him on this fourth book we have accomplished together.

To Stephen B. Hulley, M.D., Elizabeth Brodersen, Sadja Greenwood, M.D., Sally Olsen, Ph.D., Phyllis Jenkins, Ph.D., Kyra Minninger, M.D., and Christopher Putz, who offered invaluable substantive and editorial help.

To the loving members of my Thursday night writing group: Eileen Lemos, Stephanie Griffen, Liz McLoughlin, Sadja Greenwood, and Mary Goulding.

To Donal Noonan, Delos Putz, Colgon Schlank, Jolly West, Steven Minninger, and Ted Werfhorst, who provided me with rich examples of how men father.

To Charlotte Milton, Martha Stookey, Ruth Goetz, Mary Jane de Genaro, Elizabeth Starkey, Lucille Ueltzen, Gabrielle Hilberg, Judith Harrington, Margaret McKeon, Dorli Reeve, Anne Pepia, Sandra Shrift, Carolyn Talmadge, Eleanor Dugan, Suzanne Dudeck, Barbara Sanner, Gladys Bennett, Charlie Gerras, and John Moore, who have enriched my thinking.

—J.M.

ACKNOWLEDGMENTS

To all of the above, and also Lisa Carlson, so meticulous a copy editor and so valued a support. And also to my husband, Vic, and my sons Dana, Michael, and Paul, my mother, and all my friends, for their tolerance of my being absent from the world during the last intensive year of composition.

—B.G.

FOREWORD

By now it is apparent that with all the advances of knowledge about human development, we have not yet learned how to parent our children so that they enter life free of emotional injury. As a result, most children have been so wounded that they spend most of their adult lives getting over childhood. This tragic situation is the source of most social problems in any society. It is clear that the time has come to review and change the models which function unconsciously in all of us.

Nowhere has the void of information or the deficit of parenting been more pronounced than in the role of fathers in parenting, and, more particularly, in the development of daughters. Even the influence of fathers on sons has been considered minimal during infancy and early childhood, only taking on importance when the son was ready to separate from the mother, learn traditional masculine skills, and begin his exploration and control of the outside world.

Since the traditional understanding of daughters has been that they are spared separation from the mother and that the mother is the object of their identification, the father's role in the development of girls has seemed virtually nonexistent. Over the generations, the result for both sons and daughters has been "father hunger," a watchword of the emerging men's movement and a new understanding, offered in this book, of the psychology of women.

The status quo of societal roles was reinforced by modern psychological ideas, most notably those influenced by psychoanalytic

9

theory, which accepted the role of the mother and her influence on children as the norm. There was little indication of any awareness of the influence of the absent father on the mental health of children.

Only in recent times has the role of the father in parenting been subjected to study. The results seem unanimous that the absent father has been as influential by his absence as the mother has been by her presence.

This void has been admirably addressed in *The Father-Daughter Dance*. In this fine, highly readable and illuminating book, the authors describe six dysfunctional scenarios of the "father-daughter dance," which they see not only as historical but also as archetypal. These patterns, drawn from real life and fiction, depict the negative impact of the absence of the father in the daughter's life. They theorize that all daughters, as a result of the father's emotional and physical unavailability, suffer from "father hunger" which influences their relationships to men, hence negatively impacting their marriages and their relationships with their sons. They also suggest that the father's noninvolvement in parenting reinforces the deficits in his own development of having to separate from his own mother and identify with the masculine role of his father.

In addition to describing these negative patterns and suggesting Redecision Therapy, developed by Robert and Mary Goulding, as an antidote to each, Goulter and Minninger construct, on the basis of some evidence and imagination, a seventh model of a highly functional father-daughter relationship which they see emerging in our culture. This new model, titled "Loving Father and Loving Daughter," envisages a future beyond patriarchal values in which fathers are deeply involved in the nurturing and development of their daughters, an outcome which would not only benefit future daughters and their fathers, but also bring to an end the enmity between men and women. If this were all this book offered, both in content and hope, the authors would have written a book that should be read by all fathers and daughters—perhaps to each other—as well as by all parents. But this is a landmark book which should also be read by all relationship therapists and appear on the reading lists of all schools of psychology.

But their contribution in *The Father-Daughter Dance* does not end with its therapeutic value. What is even more interesting is the underlying thesis. Starting with a sweeping historical overview that begins with the hunter-gatherer societies and ends with the traditional psychological models influenced by Freud, the authors make the case that traditional parenting styles are the result of cultural rather than biological influences.

Equally fascinating, however, is the implicit thesis that the origins of patriarchy can be traced to the same phenomenon. The mother-raised son must detach himself from the mother and devalue her; attach himself to the father, identify with his emotional remoteness, and replicate his superior and demeaning attitude toward women. The mother-raised daughter identifies with the devalued mother and develops ambivalence toward her, which she later replicates as an attitude toward herself as woman and mother. She idealizes the father as the effective person who manages the outside world, thus elevating him to a position of power and dominance.

While historically understandable in terms of the evolution of male-female roles in traditional societies, the mother-raised child is the source of the daughter's ambivalence toward the mother, the elevation of men to power and relationship avoidance, the devaluation of women, the relationship of daughters to all men, men's fear of women, and ultimately the root of the male-female conflict so endemic in marriage.

This is a luminous thesis and should be the impetus for much research into the mysterious world of male-female relationships.

Harville Hendrix, Ph.D.
Author, *Getting the Love You Want: A Guide for Couples* and *Keeping the Love You Find: A Guide for Singles*
December 1992

TO THE READER

This book is a collaboration between the two authors. Every sentence written by each has been reviewed and approved by the other. In narrating Joan Minninger's case histories, however, it has sometimes been simplest to use the first-person singular. Unless otherwise indicated, when "I" is used under such circumstances, it is Joan Minninger who is speaking.

Part One

1

INVITATION TO THE DANCE

♦

O body swayed to music, O brightening glance,
How can we know the dancer from the dance?

—William Butler Yeats,
Among School Children

The Lost Daughter

When little Pamela Hollingworth was five years old, she wandered away from her family's picnic wearing only overalls and sneakers. Over the next eight days she had nothing to eat, but kept herself alive by drinking from mountain brooks. Meanwhile four hundred rescue workers combed the White Mountain National Forest looking for her. When reunited with her father, her first words were, "Daddy, I've been waiting for you."

The Father-Daughter Dance turns the spotlight on why a trust like Pamela Hollingworth's is so often betrayed and what happens to adult daughters who are still waiting for daddy. We also investigate how fathers and daughters can find each other and approach each other when they do.

Fathers are the first men that daughters ever love. Fathers teach what men are and what sort of treatment daughters can expect from them. They give the first inkling of what the world of men expects from women. As children, daughters fight for their attention, bask in their praise, rebel against their authority, hide from their anger, weep over their rejection, delight in their smiles, and thrill to their manliness.

And what of fathers? Aren't daughters also important to men? Aren't they a profound source of joy and pain, pride and disappointment?

As a psychotherapist, I have worked with hundreds of clients of both sexes. I have seen how, for women, their sense of worth-as-a-woman and worth-as-a-person is rooted in their experience of their fathers. I have observed them re-enact their struggles with their fathers, over and over, with other men. I have seen that even absent fathers have influence—that their absence *is* their influence.

I have also treated men in torment over the breakdown of their relations with their daughters, blaming themselves for their daughter's unhappiness, while blaming their daughters for their unwillingness to forgive.

Father Hunger

It's been a common assumption among mental health professionals that the mother is the crucial parent. The theory goes something like this. Young children are with their mother most of the time. According to how she treats them, they learn that the world is a supportive place where their needs will be met, or a harsh and alien environment. Later on, the father becomes important as a role model for the boys. But since the mother provides the role model for girls, fathers are not important for daughters.

It was easy enough to believe this in the days when families were still intact. Whatever contributions fathers made were taken for granted, invisible. But, starting in the sixties, the family as an institution began breaking up. Divorce rates soared, along with births to unmarried mothers, and great numbers of children started growing up fatherless. It was like a huge experiment in life without father, with society itself as the laboratory. Our own experience and observation told us to expect explosive effects, but so far, if they had occurred, they had not been acknowledged.

Then, quite suddenly, as the eighties turned to the nineties, a flood of books about fathers began to appear.[1] It was as if, at a single critical moment, the pain all around us had reached such proportions that it was no longer possible to suppress it.

One after another, important women authors like Germaine Greer, Kate Millett, and Gloria Steinem published books which revealed their childhood abandonment by their fathers. At the same time, novelists Gail Godwin and Mona Simpson came out with important father-daughter novels. Yet there was something strange about all these books. They shared common themes, yet treated them as if they were, in Scott Fitzgerald's phrase, "merely personal."

The books by male authors took a broader view. Men's movement writers, such as Robert Bly and Sam Keen, along with psychologist John Bradshaw, popularized the concept of "father hunger," arguing that boys who grow up without fathers never get over the loss.[2] Voices from the ghetto linked the chaos in the streets to growing up fatherless. "A mother can teach a boy a lot of things," said rapper Ice Cube, "but she can't teach him how to be a man."[3] Yet few of the spokesmen for men considered the effect of poor fathering on daughters.

It was statisticians who revealed the true depth and breadth of the loss, in its impact on children, girls as well as boys, from newborns to teens. Early in 1992, Louis Sullivan, Director of Health and Human Services, summarized the findings:

> Children with a missing parent are . . . five times more likely to be poor and twice as likely to drop out of school . . . Approximately 70 percent of juveniles in long-term correctional facilities did not live with their father growing up . . . Even after controlling for age, sex, race and socio-economic status, children from disrupted families were 20 to 40 percent more likely to suffer health problems than children living with

both biological parents . . . The mortality rate of infants born to college-educated but unmarried mothers is higher than for infants born to married high school dropouts.[4]

And that wasn't all. Outstanding academic psychologists, like Jay Belsky, Laurence Steinberg, and Eleanor E. Macoby, were suggesting that some fatherless girls may menstruate, have sex, and get pregnant earlier than girls with fathers in the home.[5] In *Father Hunger*, Dr. Margo Maine linked inadequate fathering with eating disorders, such as anorexia, which mostly affect adolescent girls.[6]

Who would ever have imagined that fathers could be that important to their daughters? No one, perhaps, except for the daughters themselves.

A Therapist's View

Family suffering feels very personal and is very personal, and can only be dealt with on a personal basis. Yet once we grasp that our problems are rooted in something bigger than our own individual shortcomings, it becomes easier to understand them. Having a bad father-daughter relationship these days is like getting laid off during a recession. Millions of others are in the same boat, so we know it's not our own personal fault. Yet, at the same time, like the unemployed, we have to take individual responsibility for what becomes of us in the future.

If you're a daughter, this book will help you understand why your father treated you as he did, how you were affected, and what you can do either to get over your hurt and anger or to increase the love you feel. If you're a father, you will become more aware of your own behavior, of your daughter's needs and problems as a woman, and of what you can do to win back her trust and enhance her love. If you're a father and daughter sharing this book together, you have already made an important step toward healing your relationship.

How the Trouble Began

Today's fathers and daughters are fellow victims of a crisis in human history, a drastic change in beliefs and values amounting to a revolution. To get through this crisis without its wrecking us, we need to understand what created it. This means looking back a long way.

In prehistoric times, before people discovered that sex causes babies, women dominated the family. Since the mother was the only parent her children knew, she was the one they loved and obeyed. Incredible as this idea may seem, strong circumstantial evidence supports it.

In many places, this "matriarchal" family system survived largely intact into historical times. Less than two thousand years ago in Japan, for instance, the Sun Goddess still reigned in heaven while mothers reigned at home.[7] Children of the same mother were considered sisters and brothers, but children of the same father were not. Married women lived on with their birth families. Their husbands either moved in with them or came around for visits. Some women had more than one husband. Paternity mattered little because property passed from mother to daughter.

Many similar customs have been described by explorers both ancient and modern. Some lasted until anthropologists were able to study them formally in the twentieth century.

Why is it important to know this? Because the idea of the father-dominated family is so firmly imbedded in our culture that many of us can't imagine any other kind. Yet the male-dominated family is no more natural than the female-dominated family that preceded it. Both probably came about, at least in part, because of early misunderstandings about reproduction.

Before people understood about seeds, it was thought that the earth spontaneously and miraculously brought forth life each year, and women brought forth children in the same way. The earth was like a mother and a mother was like the earth. The mother was the

21

one and only true parent, and therefore an object of awe and the source of authority.

Then, gradually, at different times in different places, the function of the seed was discovered. Unfortunately, what happened next was not a case of an ignorant idea being replaced by a factual one, but of an ignorant idea being replaced by another just as ignorant. The idea of the sole-parent father replaced that of the sole-parent mother.

The Bible referred to a man's children as his "seed." In Greece, influential thinkers like Aristotle promoted the same notion. In his play, *The Furies (Eumenides)*, Aeschylus dramatized up-to-date thinking of the fifth century B.C. Prince Orestes kills his mother in revenge for her killing his father, who had killed their daughter as a sacrifice to the gods. Orestes is pursued by the Furies, female spirits who punish those who fail to honor the mother.

The Furies is all about which family members do and don't have the right to kill each other. At the end, the god Apollo steps in to save Orestes, educate the audience, and put the Furies out of business. Fathers can kill daughters and sons can kill mothers, Apollo explains, but mothers can't avenge daughters. Why? Because *there is no parent-child relationship between mother and child, only between father and child.* Apollo declares:

> The mother is no parent to the child that is called hers, but merely the nurse of the growing seed. The parent is the planter of the seed, the one who mounts.[8]

The Furies dramatizes the triumph of patriarchy over the previous worship of the mother, justifying the revolution by an appeal to what was then the latest scientific theory—that the seed is the source of life and the male is the source of the seed. The notion of father-as-life-giver and mother-as-mere-incubator went on to dominate social thought for well over two thousand years. When sperm were first observed under the microscope in the seventeenth century, it was assumed that each held a *homunculus*—a complete little person. Drawings of sperm cells with whole babies inside were included in anatomy books well into the eighteenth century.

So, from being the sole parent, the mother was demoted to being no parent at all. Children now took the father's name and were considered members of his family, not hers. In ancient Greece as in modern China, the father decided whether a newborn was to live or die, and continued to have life-or-death powers even over an adult child. In cases of divorce or separation, men almost always kept the children. Even in America today, fathers are granted custody in at least 70 percent of the cases when they actively seek it.[9] Nor is it that fathers only sue for custody when the case against the mother is very strong. To the contrary, in *Mothers on Trial*, Phyllis Chesler marshals convincing evidence that fathers often seek custody for reasons of revenge and that mothers are judged by far more demanding standards than fathers.

The War Between the Sexes

How did men achieve this dominance? We know that in Japan it happened in a relatively slow, gradual, evolutionary way. Elsewhere, men and women literally fought it out. Greek legends about Amazons commemorate what may have been ancient battles. In Tierra del Fuego, at the tip of South America, the Ona tribes were still matriarchal when the Europeans arrived. Having seen how the Europeans did things, however, the Ona men rose up and killed all the adult women, saving only the little girls for future brides.[10] In struggles such as these, the men's superior size and strength would have been decisive.

So the "war between the sexes" was sometimes a literal war, and it didn't end with the victory. Early patriarchal literature often portrays women as dangerous deceivers who would destroy mankind if given the chance. Eve was such a woman, and so was Pandora. Training a daughter meant indoctrinating her with such an overwhelming sense of inferiority and defeat that she would never dare challenge the rule of man again.

23

Sometimes this was done directly, through threats, punishment, overwork, confinement, or by keeping women ignorant. Sometimes it was done subtly, by raising them to be helpless and ornamental. Either way, it left women feeling incapable of changing their inferior status.

The Coming of the Present Crisis

As the centuries passed, patriarchy became second nature, its values and attitudes shaping every mind. Legend and literature, customs and laws, all perpetuated male dominance. Women bore men's children, so of course they stayed home and tended them. Men were stronger and wiser, so of course they ran the world. Fathers knew best and daughters obeyed them. Anything else would have seemed preposterous.

Then, in the West, in the eighteenth century, the democratic ideal of freedom and equal justice and the pursuit of happiness began to flourish. Like slavery, the suppression of women was incompatible with this new ideal. Within a century or two, both slaves and women were set free. They ceased to be property and became citizens, but only second-class citizens.

Today, in the West, women possess the same rights as men, at least on paper. Yet they are still hampered by traditional prejudices regarding their ability, their character, and their proper place. In the United States, they receive only about 70 percent of the pay that men get for comparable jobs, while the so-called "glass ceiling" keeps them out of the top positions in government and industry.

To those fighting in the name of the democratic ideal, this progress toward true equality may seem painfully slow. From the historical vantage point, however, the change has come with stunning speed, much too fast for imbedded attitudes to keep pace.

Today, laws and professed beliefs pull us in one direction, while old feelings and customs pull us in another. Women and men are both changing, but at different rates and unevenly. Heads, hearts, and habits are all in conflict. Many women demand equal opportunity at work, yet still dream of being taken care of. Many men think they believe in equality, yet stubbornly defend their traditional advantages. The two sexes keep changing the rules on each other, driving each other so crazy sometimes that they drive each other away.

Fathers and daughters bear the full brunt of these changes. The patriarchal father was the most powerful member of the household whereas the daughter was the least powerful. This difference colored every aspect of their relationship, and still colors it today.

Daughters still learn their formative lessons about men and male-female relationships from their early experience of their fathers. The same issues that arise between the young daughter and her father recur between the adult daughter and her lovers, husbands, employers, and male managers. Everything in a daughter's life depends on resolving her father-daughter conflicts. If she can make sense of that relationship, she has a tremendous head start. But given the historical context, how many daughters can make sense of it?

The Idea of the Good Father

Many grown daughters today are furious at their fathers for not preparing them for the real world. But the world has changed drastically over the last twenty or thirty years. How could yesterday's father have known what his daughters would face today? How can today's father prepare his daughters for tomorrow?

It's not only the daughter's world that has been transformed. It's the father's too. What makes a father a good father, especially when it comes to daughters? In the two hundred years since the rise of the democratic ideal, the answer to that question has changed astonishingly.

Two hundred years ago, everyone understood what a good father was supposed to do. The father of a son was expected to:

1. protect and provide for him during childhood;
2. discipline and punish him;

3. provide a model of manhood;
4. educate him to earn a living.

The education of a girl was her mother's business. The father had only to:

1. protect and provide until he married her off;
2. discipline and punish her.

One hundred years ago, the effects of democracy were being felt. The father's relationship with his son was almost unchanged, but the daughter had become a different person. In America at least, girls were playing tennis and riding bicycles and going out on dates without a chaperon. Some had jobs before marriage, while others went to college and had careers. But the vast majority of daughters still expected to spend their adult lives as economically dependent wives-and-mothers, so fathers could still raise them in the traditional manner.

Even fifty years ago, fathers were still reasonably sure what their job entailed. At least, Billy Bigelow was.

Billy Bigelow's Fantasy Children

Rodgers and Hammerstein's *Carousel* debuted on Broadway in 1945. The first act closes with the "Soliloquy," sung by the hero, Billy Bigelow. A newly married carousel barker, Billy has just learned he is going to be a father. The "Soliloquy" expresses his feelings.

Billy first imagines a son, named for himself. He envisions young Bill growing up tall, straight, and strong, like a tree. He then pictures him in a variety of jobs from peddler to president, but never anything but tough, independent, and defiant of authority. Finally, he imagines himself teaching young Bill how to charm the girls.

That stops him. What if "Bill" should be a girl? At the thought

26

of having a daughter instead of a son, Billy is overwhelmed with grief and confusion. What on earth would he do with a daughter? As he thinks about it, however, the idea becomes more appealing. A son would be fun, but a daughter would be almost better in a way. Sweet and small, a lovely miniature of her mother, she would be someone to cherish, someone who would always need him.

He is suddenly filled with resolution. His daughter deserves care and sheltering, the best of everything, and he must get it for her, even if he has to go out and steal to do it! (In fact, he does plan a robbery, and is killed in the attempt.)

Carousel is set in the late nineteenth century, so many of its sentiments were intended to seem a bit old-fashioned. At the same time, the audience of 1945 was expected to find these sentiments congenial, and did. Certainly, Billy's images of the ideal son and daughter were both traditional and pervasive, and strongly emphasized differences over similarities.

Chronic Culture Shock

It does seem clear that our notions about what a girl should be and how a father should raise her have changed more over the last fifty years than over the previous hundred and fifty, or the thousand and fifty before that. Is it any wonder that fathers and daughters are suffering such confusion and conflict?

Today's father knows, as Billy Bigelow did not, that daughters need the same thing that sons need: not spoiling, but survival skills. At the same time, a father can't raise a daughter exactly as he raises a son, either. The choices, obstacles and opportunities facing a woman are different from those facing a man. Besides, let's be honest. What father—or mother, for that matter—doesn't secretly cherish images, like Billy Bigelow's, of strong sturdy sons and dainty, dependent daughters? Such images may not be "politically correct" anymore, but that doesn't stop a lot of people from cherishing them.

So although our heads may reject the old patriarchal roles, our hearts may still feel their pull. When we try to imagine what should replace them, consensus is hard to find. Like the poet Tennyson, we seem to be stuck between a world that is dying and another that is helpless to be born. Fortunately, when it comes to healing our personal relationships, we don't have to wait for the new world to appear.

The Danger and the Opportunity

The Chinese character for *crisis* combines the symbols for *danger* and *opportunity*. It's a perfect description of our situation today.

The *danger* is obvious. The revolution in values has made it impossible for family members to get along in the old, familiar ways. As a result, the divorce rate soars, men abandon their families, and children feel an insecurity that may well haunt them all their lives. Some of us may even conclude that we have lost more than we have gained and yearn for a return to the past. Yet we can't go back. It was democracy, after all, that killed the patriarchy. Unless we are willing to give up our ideals of freedom, equal justice, and the pursuit of happiness, the only way to go is forward.

Both matriarchy and patriarchy were one-parent families, based on false ideas. Today, we can start over with truth on our side. Today, we know that children inherit their genes from both parents equally, and that children of both sexes are most likely to flourish if they have two parents active in their lives. The hope is that whatever new family structures we create will be built on that firmly egalitarian foundation.

Our purpose, then, must be to grasp the *opportunity* and start building these new relationships *now*, in our own private lives. But before we can start building, we have to clear away the rubble. Today, we're all like survivors of a great earthquake or fire. We can't start putting up the new city until we've cleaned out the ruins of the old.

The "Opposite" Sex

One particularly troublesome piece of rubble is the patriarchal notion that men and women are opposites. Early in patriarchal times, men claimed all the admirable traits for themselves and then assigned the inverse to women. Men considered themselves strong, active, dominant, mature, protective, wise, rational, controlled, just, truthful, brave, intellectual, aspiring, spiritual, virtuous, and bright and clear as the sun. Women were therefore deemed weak, passive, submissive, childish, dependent, foolish, emotional, hysterical, sentimental, devious, cowardly, unthinking, small-minded, instinctual, treacherous, and dim and changeable as the moon. The social roles of both were imagined to be determined by their supposedly opposite natures.

As the psychoanalytic theorist Dr. Jessica Benjamin observed in a 1992 speech at the American Psychoanalytic Association Symposium, "Love, insofar as it is about knowing or embracing the other, always involves the relation to someone not only as a love object but as a like subject."[1] That is, each party has to see the other as being enough like him- or herself for mutual understanding to be possible. People who define themselves only by their differences can't have that sort of empathy. They may desire and try to possess each other as objects. They may develop all sorts of mutual fantasies and obsessions. But they can't truly know, love, or trust each other.

A father strongly influenced by patriarchal notions has a difficult time parenting a girl. Like Billy Bigelow, he perceives his son as being a creature like himself, a natural companion. But when imagining a daughter, his first response may be to consider, like Billy, what he can possibly do with her. Not knowing the answer, he may neglect, abandon, exploit, or abuse his child. Or he may make a pampered pet of her, imagining that's what she wants, and sometimes being stunned when she is ungrateful or resentful in return.

Freud's exasperated question, "What do women want?" is an

expression of exactly this attitude. For Freud, as for Billy Bigelow, women were alien, therefore incomprehensible. Billy would never have asked about a son, "What can I do with him?" Freud would never have rhetorically demanded, "What do men want?"

The small daughter of a patriarchal father soon learns that Daddy's gender is far more respected and admired than her own and that he takes her brothers more seriously. It seems natural, therefore, for her to idealize him, to try to win his attention, and to value herself according to how much he seems to value her. The father represents grown-up independence from the mother, which girls as well as boys desire. As Jessica Benjamin points out, the father is the one who either encourages or discourages the child to develop the capacity to feel desire, to *want* as an individual, rather than to merely *need* as a helpless infant.[12]

Many women in therapy seem to have stifled their capacity for desire at an early age. They may wish they were prettier or thinner or younger, but mainly because that would make them more desirable to men. They may wish to have money or possessions or to be loved or married, but most of that is associated with the longing to be taken care of. They may want to have babies because that's what women are supposed to want, or because otherwise they will have failed to meet the expectations of others. All these are desires that put them in a passive role.

The kind of desire this type of woman lacks is the active, passionate drive to practice an art, a sport, or a profession, to visit Florence or Kyoto, to backpack through the Canadian Rockies, to sit at the feet of some great teacher, to raise able and independent children, or even see her favorite team win the pennant. Such women find life essentially empty and don't know what to do with themselves. In most cases, their troubles can be traced back to a father who failed to support and validate his daughter's desires, but imposed his own will upon her.

The patriarchal insistence that common human traits be divided up between the sexes creates mutual alienation and bewilderment. As Jessica Benjamin emphasized in her speech, it creates a barrier between the sexes and thwarts the wish for "identificatory" love—the sort of love in which the parties can empathize with each other as two of a kind. More commonly, fathers and daughters view each other as "the Other."[13] Fathers, because of their greater physical and social power, enforce whatever level of relationship they please and the daughter is left to make the best of it.

Until recently, psychologists of both sexes followed Freud in taking the patriarchal division of traits for granted. Today, in the words of psychoanalyst Owen Renik, M.D., more and more mental-health professionals are stressing the importance of "the cultural surround, and how the self-images of developing boys and girls are shaped by the norms and values they pick up from their nuclear families and from the society at large."[14]

They, and we, still make use of Freud, but very selectively. Freud discovered that much of our behavior is driven by unconscious thoughts and that by bringing the unconscious to consciousness, we can achieve better mental health and change the course of our lives. This great insight permeates *The Father-Daughter Dance*. The patterns of behavior that we will be describing are all largely unconscious. By making them conscious, it becomes possible to get free of their domination.

Archetypal Father-Daughter Patterns

In *Chocolate Pudding and Other Approaches to Intensive Multiple-Family Therapy*, psychotherapist Ruth McClendon and psychiatrist Dr. Leslie B. Kadis define dysfunctional relationships as those in which "patterns are limited in number, shallow in depth, and rigidly adhered to."[15] By this standard, most patriarchal father-daughter relationships have been dysfunctional. Because of the power gap between them, fathers and daughters learned to behave together in patterns that were "shallow in depth, and rigidly adhered to."

These patterns were also "limited in number." Whether we look in ancient myths and legends, in modern fiction and drama, in the biographies of famous people, or in the case histories of therapy clients, we see that six patterns keep appearing again and again:

1. Lost Father and Yearning Daughter

In this relationship, the father abandons the daughter, either by outright desertion or by rejection, remoteness, or neglect. The daughter becomes obsessed with trying to understand his reasons, or with blaming her own shortcomings, or with struggling to earn his acceptance, or with desperately seeking a father surrogate.

2. Abusive Father and Victim Daughter

In this relationship, the father persecutes his daughter through physical, emotional, or sexual abuse. The daughter identifies herself as a victim and grows up seeking other relationships in which she can play victim and/or rescuer and/or persecutor.

3. Pampering Father and Spoiled Daughter

In this relationship, the father makes a pet of his daughter, giving her everything she asks for, and more, without requiring her to earn it. The daughter learns to control others through charm or temper, yet lacks inner control and a sense of personal competence.

4. Pygmalion Father and Companion Daughter

In this relationship, the father mentors his daughter, molding her into an exceptionally able woman and his ideal companion. The daughter grows up feeling special and privileged, yet believing that she owes it all to her father and would be nothing without him.

5. Ruined Father and Rescuing Daughter

In this relationship, a previously distant father turns to his daughter when he is in trouble, expecting her to take care of him. The daughter sacrifices her own well-being in order to win his approval and prove her value to him.

6. Anguished Father and Angry Daughter
In this relationship, the daughter cultivates a lasting enmity against her father, deliberately punishing him however she can and rejecting him when he is in need.

Don't be surprised if you can't recognize your own relationship among these six. If patterns were pure or self-recognition easy, there would be no need for us to write this book. Most of us take the norms of our culture for granted, as being natural, and family members are seldom aware of playing roles. Indulgent fathers seldom think of themselves as spoiling their daughters, but as providing well; abusive fathers often see their children as "asking for it." In a similar way, companion daughters may feel too privileged to realize that they are being demeaned, while most angry daughters are convinced that they are responding appropriately to paternal mistreatment.

Also, because times have been changing so rapidly, some of today's fathers and daughters may think they have escaped the influence of patriarchal tradition. In some cases, that may be so. For most people, however, it's hard to live immersed in a powerful tradition and not absorb more of it than they realize. As you proceed through *The Father-Daughter Dance*, be alert for examples that strike a familiar chord. These will indicate which pattern or patterns have been affecting your father-daughter relationship. Remember, the purpose of acknowledging your own patterns is not to put yourself into a pigeonhole, but to allow you more conscious control over your life.

In Part One of *The Father-Daughter Dance*, we will be exploring these six patterns, with examples from life, legend, fiction, film, and case histories. We will see how this sort of patterned behavior inhibits spontaneity and responsiveness, and how it prevents fathers and daughters from getting to know themselves or each other. We will also see how rigid and predictable these patterns are, and how much the daughter's steps are controlled by the father's.

In a way, these patterns are like ballroom dance routines, with the man leading, the girl following, and only a very few stereotyped movements allowed. A generation or two ago, there used to be special proms, mainly at schools or churches, which fathers and daughters attended together. These were called *father-daughter dances.* Even today, at weddings and other special occasions, fathers and daughters are sometimes expected to dance together. To the casual eye, such couples may seem to be getting on beautifully. But reality often belies appearances.

The father-daughter dance at a school or wedding mercifully comes to an end. But the psychological father-daughter dance never ends unless the partners find a way to end it. Otherwise, the couple goes on compulsively, like the girl in the *Ballet of the Red Shoes,* dancing the same steps for as long as they live.

Part Two of *The Father-Daughter Dance* offers a way to take the compulsion out of the dancing. The poet Yeats implied that we cannot know the dancer from the dance. In reality, it's urgently important to make the distinction. Otherwise, we spend our lives going through the motions instead of learning and growing. Fathers and daughters do *not* have to stay locked in their limited, shallow, rigid patterns. They can stop the dance and can learn to be real together—or at least stop making demands that the other cannot meet.

Parent and child are not natural enemies. Underneath our accumulated frustrations, we fathers and daughters do love each other. The goal of *The Father-Daughter Dance* is to help clear away the barriers, so that we can flourish in the light of that love.

2

THE LOST FATHER AND HIS YEARNING DAUGHTER

◆

> All you have to do to become somebody's
> god is to disappear.
>
> —Mona Simpson, *The Lost Father*

The Lost Father

In 1991, author Camille Paglia published a column about two women writers who had flourished in the 1970s but whose careers she now saw as in decline.[1] Susan Sontag and Germaine Greer had both made such a great start, she said. Why had they not fulfilled their promise?

At first glance, this might seem a pointless question. Plenty of people in every field make a great start then slump. Besides, Susan Sontag had been seriously ill, and both women had many years left in which to produce major works.

But Camille Paglia is one of those provocative and sometimes outrageous thinkers who love to play with theories to see what they will yield. Germaine Greer and Susan Sontag, she observed, had both grown up father-deprived. As young women, they had seemed not to feel the loss, but the older they grew, the more it appeared to affect them, Germaine Greer especially. In her youth, she had written *The Female Eunuch*, a feminist study bursting with fresh ideas. In her middle age, she produced *Daddy, We Hardly Knew You*, a highly personal account of her search through her father's family history.

Camille Paglia then asked a question. What if these two women had stopped generating new ideas because the loss of their fathers had hurt them more than they knew? Actually, she might have included a third feminist star in the question. Kate Millett, whose *Sexual Politics* had once been so influential, had only recently published *The Loony Bin Trap*, the history of her long years spent battling mental illness, poverty, and a father-obsession. Her father, a charming but bankrupt alcoholic, had abandoned the family when she was thirteen, and she had just spent many years in a failed attempt to write a book about him.

And more corroboration was to come. In 1992, Gloria Steinem published *Revolution from Within,* her first book in almost a decade. Here was another feminist writer switching from public to personal issues. And what was a crucial event in Gloria Steinem's girlhood? While still a child, she had been abandoned by her father, leaving her to cope with her emotionally disturbed mother alone.

Revolution from Within became an overnight best-seller. In the same month, Mona Simpson's *The Lost Father,* a compelling novel about an abandoned daughter, was published. It was as if the whole father-daughter issue had suddenly come out of the closet. Perhaps it was true that—for all their theories about the oppressiveness of the male presence—at least part of what had always been driving writers like Germaine Greer and Kate Millett and Gloria Steinem, and maybe a lot of other women too, was really the oppressiveness of the male absence. Maybe, like hurt, angry children, they had been crying out loud, "I hate you. Who needs you? Get the hell out of my life," while all the time in their hearts they were sobbing, "I love you. I need you. Please come back."

The Song of the Road

Powerful ties bind fathers and daughters, even if they have never met. The story of abandoned daughters in search of their fathers is one of the most ancient and widespread in the world. Mayan Stevenson in *The Lost Father* is only the latest of many such heroines—actual, fictional, and legendary.

In some of these stories, the girl finds her father, only to be rejected again. In others, she tries to compensate for his loss with a substitute, or many substitutes. In still others, she comes upon him just as he discovers his need for her, and they have an improbably joyful reunion.

It's really no wonder that there should be so many such stories. The hard, cold, statistical fact is that fathers are far more likely to desert daughters than sons.

Marilyn Monroe and the Repetition Compulsion

The late Barney Ruditsky was a top Hollywood private detective whose adventures were the basis for a TV detective series, *The Lawless Years.* Insiders jokingly called him "Wrong-Door Ruditsky." Barney had earned this nickname after being hired by one of Marilyn Monroe's husbands to break in on her while she was with a lover at a motel.[2] Because he was fond of Marilyn, felt sorry for her, and didn't want to see her publicly humiliated, Barney accidentally-on-purpose broke in on the room next door instead.

According to Barney, Marilyn had hired detectives to trace the father who had abandoned her before she was born. She was certainly looking for his substitute all her life. Born out of wedlock and raised in foster homes, she sought out powerful, protective, larger-than-life men: sports hero Joe DiMaggio, playwright Arthur Miller, French superstar Yves Montand, President John F. Kennedy, Attorney General Robert Kennedy.

All but DiMaggio were already married. Going after a family man is usually a no-win situation for the woman in search of a father. If the married man's a good enough father, he'll give the woman up for the sake of his family. If he gives up his family for her sake, then he's probably not such a good father. She loses either way.

Of all Marilyn's lovers, only Arthur Miller gave up his family for her. On paper, he looked like everything a father should be. He was older; he was dignified and successful; he was eager to mentor her education; he could even gain her acceptance in intellectual circles. Yet she drove him so crazy with her moods and infidelities that he, too, abandoned her. After that, she set herself up for further abandonment by becoming involved with John and Robert Kennedy, both married and neither in a position to acknowledge their relationship.

Marilyn's story is like a textbook illustration of the *repetition compulsion*—the need to act out our unconscious conflicts, to keep replaying the unfinished business of our lives until either we work it out or it destroys us. It's the repetition compulsion that writes our unhappy "life scripts," that dictates our unwise decisions, that keeps confronting us with just the sorts of people and situations that we consciously wish to avoid. It's the repetition compulsion that sometimes makes our lives feel so "fated," and that accounts for the fact that a powerful early experience—like the loss of a father—can create lifelong difficulties.

There is an old saying that we can never get enough of what we don't really want. The child who became Marilyn Monroe never had the attention of the one man who mattered. Grown up, she made a career of attracting men by the millions. But the adoration of fans and even the lust of lovers can't make up for the protective, unconditional devotion of a father. Marilyn was too desperate for love to be able to give love, yet the repetition compulsion kept her on the treadmill.

Three Orphans in Search of a Father

The search for the father does not always end tragically. Sometimes a fatherless daughter will find a substitute "daddy," or else she will discover the resources within herself that allow her to end her quest.

During the same years when Marilyn Monroe was coming to womanhood, three other beautiful girls her age were also growing up without fathers.[3] They called themselves "the orphans" and remained lifelong intimate friends. We can now look back over the course of their lives to see how their fathers' absence affected them.

The first thing we notice is that the "orphans" were never much interested in "boys." Even at fifteen or sixteen, they were attracted to "men"—much, much older men.

Oona—Daddy's Girl

Oona O'Neill, daughter of the great playwright Eugene O'Neill, was one of the three "orphans." When Oona was two years old, her father walked out on the family. Oona saw her famous father no more than half a dozen times before she reached her teens. When he did arrange to see her, it wasn't to make things up to her. Instead, he forbade her to "exploit" his name, warned her away from a theatrical career, advised her to take up nursing, and disowned her when she was eighteen.

There was no way Oona could forget this brutally rejecting father, for even a day. His name was constantly in the news and up in lights on Broadway. Because of who *he* was, *she* was eagerly welcomed into the highest circles of New York society. She was probably the least wealthy girl ever to be named "Debutante of the Year."

At eighteen, the gloriously beautiful Oona married fifty-three-year-old Charles Chaplin, known to the world as *Charlie*. By all accounts, it was an extraordinarily happy marriage, lasting thirty-four years and producing eight children. Charles and Oona were inseparable, even symbiotic. When she needed clothes, he waited outside in the limousine while she ran into a shop and grabbed things off the rack.[4] They often held hands, gazing into each other's eyes and laughing together.

Charlie Chaplin and Eugene O'Neill had an amazing amount in common. Both had been raised in show-business families by mentally disturbed mothers and alcoholic fathers. Both had a history of failed marriages and were known to be domineering, egotistical, and moody. Both were world-famous theatrical geniuses. The difference was that Charlie adored Oona and wanted her with him every minute. He was the perfect father-substitute, and Oona spent her womanhood having the childhood she'd never had. As before, she derived her identity from the fame of a man. As a girl, she had been "Eugene O'Neill's daughter." As a woman, she was "Charlie Chaplin's wife."

It was not until Charlie died that the price had to be paid for such symbiosis. Just past fifty, healthy and still very beautiful, immensely rich, a friend of the most famous and fascinating people of the day, with a minor child or two left to raise and grandchildren now coming, Oona O'Neill Chaplin had no will to live. She spent the rest of her days in seclusion, mainly in the bedroom that she had shared with Charlie, the draperies drawn. As she confided to her fellow "orphan," Carol Marcus, it was "nice" to make the room as cool and dark and silent as her husband's grave.[5]

Emotionally dependent on her "fathers," Oona apparently never achieved an independent personal identity. Abandoned again, all she could do was wait for death.

Carol—Cinderella Twice Over

Carol Marcus, the second of the "orphans," didn't even know who her father was. Most of her first eight years were spent in foster care. Then her mother married an industrial tycoon and suddenly the abandoned child found herself living in splendor on Park Avenue with marble floors, eighteen servants, and a kindly "Daddy."

Her new daddy treated her like his own child, yet Carol could not feel secure in his love. Her mother was afraid to tell him that Carol wasn't her only child, that she had another daughter still in foster care. Carol helped her mother keep the secret, both dreading that if the truth came out, their wonderful new life would disappear like Cinderella's coach at midnight. It was two years before her mother confessed the truth to her stepfather and Carol's little sister came to live with them.

For all her early difficulties, Carol grew up to be a stunning, clever, sparkling young woman. Like Oona, she was married at eighteen—to William Saroyan, the world-famous writer, twice her age.

Their glamorous wedding was followed by a nightmare marriage. As his career declined and his wealth disappeared, Bill Saroyan took to abusing and demeaning his wife. Despite bearing two children, publishing a novel, and playing featured roles on Broadway, Carol felt like a worthless nothing and even contemplated suicide. She endured a hellish life for over ten years, divorcing her husband twice, yet unable to make a final break.

Carol's confidante during these years was Gloria Vanderbilt. Her life, Carol told Gloria, consisted of "living off someone else's smile."[6] Without Bill's approval she felt she would stop existing, so she continued the hopeless struggle to please him.

Carol's adult life, like Marilyn's and Oona's, repeated the patterns of her childhood. She had felt like a helpless, rejected victim while in foster care. She felt like a helpless, rejected victim again, married to William Saroyan. Later, the pattern of a fairy-tale rescue by a loving daddy was also repeated. Into her life came Walter Matthau, then relatively poor and unknown but kindly and protective. He helped her break from William Saroyan, and they married for love, only to have him skyrocket to fame and fortune soon afterward. So, once again, Carol Marcus found herself rich and pampered through no effort of her own. This time her luck held, and Cinderella actually did live happily ever after.

Gloria—The Waif

"Orphan" number three was Gloria Vanderbilt, whose father had died when she was just a year old. Gloria missed having a father so much that she actually envied her friend Oona O'Neill. As she recollects in her autobiography, *Black Knight, White Knight*, having even a heartless father like Oona's was "better than having no father at all."[7]

Gloria had spent her early childhood being carried from hotel to villa to ship to train in the wake of her rootless playgirl of a mother. Then her widowed aunt, a sculptor, sued for custody and won, separating Gloria from both her mother and her beloved nurse, Dodo. The media called Gloria "the poor little rich girl" and pictured her as no better than a waif—homeless and subjected to agonizing separations.

Gloria yearned for a home of her own and a family life. After a brief, unsuccessful teenage marriage, the twenty-one-year-old Gloria wed the world-famous conductor, Leopold Stokowski, aged sixty-three. "I'm protected for as long as he loves me,"[8] she imagined. "Soon, very soon now, everything that happened long ago— all the ugliness—will be erased because he loves me."[9] For the first time in her life, she confided to her diary, she did not have to wake up every day feeling afraid.

Gloria wanted what Oona already had, closeness with her aging genius husband and a baby every year. Unfortunately, once again, Oona's apparent blessings were denied to Gloria.

Like Gloria's mother, her new husband was a person who couldn't settle down. Leopold Stokowski's career took him on a continual round of concert tours, all over the globe. In those prejet days, travel was time-consuming and arduous. Early in the marriage, Gloria tried leaving her first baby at home, to go along on a tour; but the separation was too painful. Next time, she took the baby along, but the traveling was too difficult. Reluctantly, she decided to stay home with her children while her husband traveled, dooming herself to a marriage of long separations and brief reunions. And she dared not even complain, lest she "spoil" the little time they had together.

Eventually, Gloria realized that she, too, like Carol Marcus, was "living off another's smile." As a desolate eight-year-old child, deprived of her nurse, she had made a conscious decision not to kill herself or go crazy, no matter what. She now reaffirmed that decision. Talented at acting, writing, and art, she decided to make her own identity through creative work. By this means she became a survivor and was finally able to get out of her hopeless marriage.

Gloria's later marriage to Wyatt Cooper was her happiest. A man of her own generation, he gave her two more children and encouraged her career as a designer. By a strange twist of fate, Wyatt suddenly died within a week of Charlie Chaplin's death, so that Gloria and Oona became widows simultaneously. Gloria, however, did not bury herself alive. Instead, she found solace in her children and her work.

Compensating for the Lost Father

Oona, Gloria, and Carol, and of course Marilyn Monroe, were among the most glamorous women of their generation. Their lives were magical in many ways, and yet fatherlessness shaped their destinies, and a vast portion of their energy went into attempts to compensate.

How well they managed seems to have been linked in some degree to how much money they had as children. Gloria, the richest, ultimately created the strongest and most independent self. Marilyn managed to overcome the most and achieve the most with the fewest advantages, yet she died a tragic early death.

This is not to say that money compensates for the lack of a father, only that the lack of money compounds the problem. The same probably applies to beauty, charm, ability, energy, luck, fame, lifelong friends, and a social network. If such gifts do not solve all problems, they do at least tend to provide more options.

The three orphans had or acquired most of life's supposed blessings, as did Marilyn Monroe, Germaine Greer, and Kate Millett. Yet, even for these unusually fortunate women, fatherlessness remained a powerful factor in their lives, sometimes canceling out their gifts of nature and fortune.

Kagekiyo's Daughter

What is it that a little girl misses when her father isn't there? What is it the grown woman seeks when she goes in quest of him?

43

In legend and story, the daughter often finds her lost father, winning his love in time for a happy ending. Perhaps the most moving embodiment of this archetypal tale is Seami's *Kagekiyo*, written in fifteenth-century Japan.[10] *Kagekiyo* is a *Noh* drama, a symbolic one-act play that uses poetry, dance, and music to express elemental emotions. *Kagekiyo* captures the essence of the lost father-yearning daughter so perfectly that it's worth describing in detail.

The play opens with the entrance of Kagekiyo's daughter, a girl on the verge of womanhood. She is on a journey to find her father, once a famous warrior, now blind, impoverished, and in exile. "I must not be downcast at the toil of the journey," she says, in Arthur Waley's powerful translation, "for hardship is the lot of all that travel on unfamiliar roads, and I must bear it for my father's sake."

She comes to a hut. Kagekiyo's voice is heard from within, lamenting his total misery. She sends in her servant to inquire for news of Kagekiyo, but gets the reply that no such person is there. The daughter continues on her search and Kagekiyo emerges from the hut.

He is almost sure the girl must be his abandoned daughter. "I courted a woman and had a child by her. But since the child was a girl, I thought I would get no good of her and left her with the headman of the valley of Kamegaye."

He had provided for her materially but abandoned her emotionally, sacrificing her to his ego and ambition. Briefly, fame and glory were his. Now they are gone. He is penitent and yearns for his daughter but is ashamed to face her as a beggar.

KAGEKIYO:
To hear a voice,
To hear and not to see!
Oh pity of blind eyes!
I have let her pass by;
I have not told my name;
But it was love that bound me,

Love's rope that held me . . .
Let them shout, "Kagekiyo, Kagekiyo":
Need beggars answer?

The girl inquires of a villager, who brings her back to the hut. The villager reproaches Kagekiyo for rejecting his child after her heroic journey.

The girl touches her father's sleeve. He does not respond, and she interprets his silence as more rejection. In tears, she implores him to acknowledge her, speaking for all father-hungry, abandoned daughters.

GIRL:
It is I who have come to you.
I have come all the way,
Through rain, wind, frost and dew.
And now—you have not understood; it was all for
    nothing.
Am I not worth your love? Oh cruel, cruel!

These words end his resistance. He can't bear for her to go away thinking that *she* is the unworthy one. He explains his reluctance to disgrace her before the world or become a burden to her.

KAGEKIYO:
Should you, oh flower delicately tended,
Call me your father, then would the World know you
A beggar's daughter. Oh think not ill of me
That I did let you pass.

The villager now speaks. The daughter, he says, wants something of her father. "She tells me she longs to hear the story of your high deeds at Yashima."

Kagekiyo offers an exchange. He will tell the story, if she will promise to leave immediately afterwards. The daughter agrees.

Their bargain contains the whole meaning of *Kagekiyo,* and we will return to it in just a moment.

Kagekiyo tells his story. It begins as a typical tale of warrior exhibitionism. Heroically, Kagekiyo drives a cowardly flock of enemy samurai up the beach. Then he reaches out to grab someone to kill and accidentally breaks off a piece of the fellow's armor instead. The intended victim gets away, and Kagekiyo looks so ridiculous holding the broken armor that both sides stop fighting to laugh. Heroism becomes absurd comedy.

Looking back, Kagekiyo now sees the famous battle as an empty spectacle of cruelty, cowardice, and farce; for whatever he had abandoned his daughter to seek, was of no value compared to her love. He bids her an awesome farewell.

KAGEKIYO:
The end is near: go to your home.
Pray for my soul departed, child, candle to my
      darkness,
Bridge to salvation!

The daughter he had once rejected has saved his soul. Thanks to her, his bitterness is gone, and he is filled with love, light, joy, and peace. She, having healed his pain and received this tribute, can go away happy. They part without another word, mutually released and mutually blessed.

The Rejected Daughter's Yearnings

Kagekiyo may have been written long ago and far away, but it is as familiar as the air we breathe. What Kagekiyo and his daughter receive from each other is what abandoned daughters and repentant fathers yearn for to this day. Let's consider the daughter's yearnings first.

The daughter wants her love to be accepted and returned. That is the driving force behind her obsessive and dangerous journey.

She wants to know she has value as a person and that it was not her fault that he went away. This is why she pleads, "Am I not worthy of your love?"

She wants to understand the attraction of what lured him away. This is one reason she asks to hear of his "great deeds at Yashima."

She wants to be able to admire him. This is another reason for wanting to hear of his "great deeds."

She wants to be able to get close to him, to share in his experience, to know vicariously through him what it means to be a man. This is yet another reason to ask for his story.

She wants to help him. Being of use puts love into action. She hopes that recalling his great deeds will restore his pride. In fact, she would like nothing better than to stay with him as long as he needs her.

She wants to know that she can be, at least for one moment, the very most important thing in his life. Kagekiyo gives her this, bountifully.

Above all, she wants to be released from her obsession, so she can find her own identity and start living her own life. By amply meeting her needs, then gently forcing her to go, Kagekiyo gives her exactly that.

The Abandoning Father's Yearnings

And what does Kagekiyo want? What does his daughter have the power to give? The answer is that he wants forgiveness and the end of entrapment within his masculine ego. But there are things he needs to do in order to get these wishes satisfied.

He needs to put aside his false pride. Kagekiyo's shame at being a beggar is so great that he almost misses his chance to meet the child he so longs for.

He needs to place his daughter's needs before his own. Kagekiyo would have missed his own chance for salvation if his pity for her had not moved him to let her stay.

He needs to fulfill her wishes even if he doesn't understand them. Kagekiyo is puzzled by her desire to hear his story, but tells it anyway.

He needs to confess his fault and to receive and return her love. Until he does so, Kagekiyo lives in bitterness, haunted by his egotistical grief over the thwarting of his ambitions.

He needs to realize that what she has to offer is the most important thing in the world. And what exactly does she have to offer? Nothing less than love, enlightenment, liberation from self, and the joy of life.

Then he needs to let her go. To do otherwise would exploit her and create a mutual dependency. Once their yearnings are fulfilled, he must set her free to live her own life.

This last idea is a very Buddhist one, and it makes for a different ending from many Western variations on the theme. As we will see later, it's much more common for stories about rescuing daughters to conclude with the daughter's total commitment to her father unto death. The modern, psychotherapeutic point of view clearly prefers the *Kagekiyo* ending. Father and daughter need to reconcile, not in order to fuse, or commit emotional incest, or turn the daughter into a servant to her father, but to allow them to lovingly separate and seek their individual destinies.

In short, Kagekiyo did for his daughter what Marilyn Monroe had hoped her father would do for her, and in fact what every daughter longs for from her father: he acknowledged her, loved her, freed her from father-obsession, and sent her off with his blessing to make a good life.

Abandonment, Home Style

Kagekiyo takes place in a dream world, an ideal realm where fathers and daughters both know the right thing to do and how to do it. In the real world, it doesn't often happen that way. In the real world, also, abandonment is not always such a clear-cut issue. A father doesn't have to disappear forever in order to leave a daughter feeling abandoned. He can do it while living in the same town, or even under the same roof.

48

"I'm my father's only daughter," a fourteen-year-old said, "but he never talks to me. If only he'd talk to me, I'd be so happy." In clinical practice, therapists have the daily experience of listening to adult women, middle-aged women, and even elderly women, whose hearts are still breaking because they never could get those few words of acknowledgment from Daddy.

The pain of living with a father who just doesn't seem to care can be as devastating as outright desertion. An abandoned girl can console herself with fantasies that her faraway father really loves and misses her. But there's no dreaming away the daily, eyewitness evidence that a father cares far more for his bottle or his book or his baseball game—or his son—than he does for his daughter.

Growing Up Father-Hungry

What happens to the father-hungry little girl as she grows up? For one thing, she will usually lack confidence in herself as a person and a woman, and fail to get rewarded in proportion to her abilities. For another, she may have a far greater-than-average craving for male attention and affection. Because she loves her father, and yearns for what he never gave her, she will tend to choose similar men: that is, men who are *less* attentive and affectionate than average. The result is a vicious circle in which she keeps craving more and more and getting less and less and having her confidence further undermined at every turn.

The result is a dynamic observed by Deborah Tannen in her book, *You Just Don't Understand: Women and Men in Conversation*. In many cases, a man will be delighted with a situation in which he and his beloved are under the same roof doing totally different things and not talking, while the woman will feel shut out and neglected. In such cases, the man takes his cue from what it was like being a child in his mother's company. Having received plenty of maternal attention, he felt content enough to pursue his interests without needing more. The woman, in contrast, takes her cue from having been a little girl in her father's company. If she was starved for his attention then, she will still feel starved now.[11]

In an address to the American Psychoanalytic Institute, Dr. Ethel Spector Person observed that what we most require from a lover is someone who can identify with and reciprocate our feelings.[12] So the man wants a woman who can be as quietly content with his presence as he is with hers. For the daughter of a distant father, however, this is virtually impossible. She craves a man who will reciprocate her unmet needs for closeness and communication, yet there are few such men around. And because she tends to choose men who are especially incapable of reciprocating, her life may easily get into a downward spiral.

Hiding from Daddy—Bernadette

As soon as Bernadette arrived for her first session of therapy she succumbed to a storm of muffled tears. Thirty years old, petite and slim, she would have been attractive if she'd had a little more spirit. Her father, an alcoholic stevedore, had little fondness for his brood of nine. He sometimes talked sports with the boys, but he treated the girls like pests and yelled at them whenever they came near. Frequently he sent Bernadette to her room. She went through childhood like a little stowaway, trying to make the journey to adulthood without being noticed.

Once grown, she worked her way through nursing school and became a nurse. When her supervisor retired, she was next in line and seemed the logical successor. But stowaways don't get invited to run the ship. Another nurse was promoted over her head.

Then Bernadette was assigned to night duty, which most of the other senior nurses had already refused. That was the last straw. "Night duty is where they send you when they don't want to be bothered with you," she sobbed, sounding just like a sad little girl who'd been sent to her room. Afraid of losing her job, she accepted the assignment, but she was dying inside. "It's just not fair!" she whimpered, very softly. She knew better than to complain aloud.

In her book, *Silencing the Self: Women and Depression*, Dana Crawley Jack explains how unwanted daughters may decide to pacify their fathers by offering no resistance and making no demands.[13] Bernadette had done exactly that, and now she was paying the price.

Showing Off for Daddy—Renee

To the casual eye, Renee was as different from Bernadette as anyone could be. Somewhat overweight, boldly dressed, and assertive in voice and manner, she came on like a human tank, rolling over everything. Yet she had no real confidence at all.

Her father had been an internationally known research scientist and chairman of his department at a top Ivy League university. Caught up in his activities, he hardly noticed Renee's existence. Renee concluded that she must not be "interesting" enough or "good" enough or "important" enough to merit his attention and made it her goal in life to become enough of everything.

She cultivated achievements and opinions and honors by the droves and paraded them at every opportunity. When she still didn't get her father's attention, she tried even harder. "Why is it that nothing I do is ever enough?" she would complain, then pull herself together for another try.

At twenty-five, Renee married Bill, a fellow graduate student working for his doctorate in physics. Over the next four years, she tried very hard to be "enough" for Bill too. She supported them both, helped with his research, coached him for his orals, and practically wrote his thesis for him. Then, doctorate in hand, Bill accused her of being a domineering bitch and walked out.

"It isn't fair!" she protested loudly, weeping angry tears. "I did everything for that man. Why wasn't it enough? Why didn't he love me? How much more can one person be expected to do?"

Renee and Bernadette were both trapped in the repetition compulsion. Faced with the daily agony of living with a rejecting father, Renee had decided to push while Bernadette had decided to withdraw. Although neither decision had paid off, each had compulsively carried her approach into adulthood, where it continued to bring her more pain.

Fortunately, both women hurt enough to be willing to enter therapy. Today, Bernadette has a supervisory job at another hospital, while Renee is remarried, teaching college, and enjoying her work without feeling that her life depends on outshining everyone.

Why Fathers Leave

Why should a father abandon a daughter, either literally or emotionally? What can he possibly hope to gain in exchange for breaking her heart and depriving himself of her love?

In some cases, the hope of gain hardly enters in, since the father starts out with a diminished capacity for parenthood.

Some men are driven by addiction, either to a substance or a lover. In Eugene O'Neill's case, it was both. Traumatized by his own agonized childhood and devastated by alcohol, he was emotionally dependent on a possessive new wife who refused to share any part of him or his money with his children. Others suffer emotional illness. According to Germaine Greer, her emotionally weak father never got over the trauma he suffered during World War II. Anorexic and despondent, he was like a ghost in the house, unable to respond to his family.

With still others, there's a serious lack of self-esteem that makes holding a job or overcoming problems exceptionally difficult. Such men feel useless as fathers. What's the use of being there for your child if you have nothing to offer but a bad example? The high level of family abandonment in our slums and ghettos is probably an effect of this syndrome.

With still others, it's an incapacity to stand up to the jealousy or possessiveness of the child's mother. Marilla remembers her father coming home each day from work with a token present—a lollipop, a subway token, a balloon—just to tell her he'd been thinking of her. She also remembers her mother throwing tantrums, accusing him of loving the child more than her, until he not only stopped bringing presents but withdrew from Marilla almost entirely.

The Kagekiyo Syndrome

Among fathers possessed of a reasonable level of mental health, it's usually the *Kagekiyo Syndrome* that takes them away. Kagekiyo, remember, absconded for three closely related reasons: because he didn't love his child's mother, because he didn't value a daughter, and because ambition and excitement and adventure were beckoning.

That pretty well describes how it must have been for young William Shakespeare. Will had been married at eighteen to a woman almost a decade his senior who was already three months pregnant, presumably by him. A daughter was born, quickly followed by twins, a boy and a girl. Next thing we know, young Will had left little Stratford for London and a life in the theater. By the age of twenty-eight, he was being celebrated both as an actor and a playwright.

Other theatrical men of the day, such as Ben Jonson, had their families with them in the city. Will Shakespeare, we know, did not. Also, despite the early death of their only son, Ann Hathaway Shakespeare never had another child.

Here was the *Kagekiyo Syndrome* in every detail: the unloved wife, the abandoned daughters, the man's yearning for self-fulfillment through the use of his talents.

In the last years before his retirement, Shakespeare wrote one play after another about fathers and daughters. In several cases, a father impulsively rejects a daughter, then lives to repent it. In *The Winter's Tale* and *Much Ado about Nothing,* a happy twist of the plot allows for a reconciliation at the end. In *King Lear,* reconciliation comes too late and both the father and his good daughter die. *King Lear* also deals with vindictive daughters eaten up by hatred of their unsatisfactory father, while *The Tempest* features a blissfully devoted father and daughter marooned for years together on a magical desert island. Plainly, William Shakespeare had some pretty significant feelings to work through.

Abandonment as a Duty

No one who cares for literature or the theater can be sorry that the young Shakespeare left Stratford for London. And no one who loves art can regret that Paul Gauguin abandoned his family to end up painting in Tahiti. On the strength of such examples, a tradition has arisen that makes it all right and even admirable for a man to sacrifice his children in the name of following his star—or simply his desires.

This tradition was receiving heavy reinforcement during the years when the fathers of the present adult generation were growing up. *The Corn Is Green,* a successful play and film of the forties, tells of a schoolteacher in Wales who discovers a gifted boy working in the coal mines. She tutors him, and he wins a university scholarship, but then a girl who seduced him one night turns up pregnant. Should he marry the girl and go back to the mines, or go on to Oxford, as planned?

The Corn Is Green comes down firmly on the side of *not* marrying the pregnant girl. She is evil, scheming, and vicious, whereas the boy has the potential for a great future. It's the boy's *duty*—to himself, to his teacher, to his family, to the townsfolk, and to other ambitious working-class lads—to become a big success. So the boy leaves the mines and the audience leaves the theater, both happy.

A Place in the Sun, a film based on Theodore Dreiser's novel *An American Tragedy,* won many awards in the early fifties. A poor but ambitious young man, played by the super-sensitive Montgomery Clift, is working his way up in his rich uncle's business. He has just become engaged to a ravishing debutante when his discarded girlfriend shows up pregnant and threatens to expose him.

In *A Place in the Sun,* as in *The Corn Is Green,* sympathy goes to the ambitious young man, not the pregnant girl. As played by Shelley Winters, she is stupid, coarse, and never stops whining.

How could any man be expected to give up the eighteen-year-old Elizabeth Taylor, and a life of luxury, to marry such a nuisance? When the Clift character sits by and allows the pregnant girl to drown, and is later convicted of her murder, the audience is filled with sadness for him, not for her.

Later in the fifties, John Updike's *Rabbit, Run* was a top best-seller. "Rabbit" Angstrom, once a high-school sports star, feels stuck with his wife and two babies. How can a man put up with a woman whose breasts smell of milk and are lined with blue veins? Rabbit's solution is to find a sexier woman and move out.

The late forties and fifties have the reputation of being a conservative period devoted to family "togetherness." Yet, even then, some male writers and filmmakers were encouraging men to see women and children as shackles and to abandon them to pursue their own goals. Even then, the domesticated "man in the gray flannel suit" was an object of satire, while lone-wolf heroes like James Dean, Marlon Brando, Elvis Presley, and Jack Kerouac were creating images of sexy, untamed male rebellion and laying the groundwork for the sixties.

A paternal father places a permanent value on his child and the child's mother. A patriarchal father values them only if they fit in with his plans. Even in the family-centered fifties, patriarchal values prevailed over paternal values.

And yet we know from *Kagekiyo* and Shakespeare's last plays, and countless other stories, too, that the man who abandons his daughter risks his soul.

3

THE ABUSIVE FATHER AND HIS VICTIM DAUGHTER

◆

Dear Beth: I am almost 11 and my father treats me like a kid. He teases me about wearing a training bra. I don't know what to do. I've tried to talk to him about it but he always ends up almost making me cry. When my period starts, I'll have even more problems. What do I do?—A Very Troubled Girl

—"Dear Beth," *San Francisco Examiner,* 21 June 1992

Dorothy

Dorothy*, a woman in her mid-thirties, attended a five-day workshop in Redecision Therapy. Here is her first piece of work.

THERAPIST: Okay, Dorothy. What do you want to change about yourself?

DOROTHY: I want to stop seeing my mother, and not feel guilty about it.

THERAPIST: Pretend your mother is here, sitting in that chair in front of you. Tell her, "I don't want to see you because . . ."

*We thank Mary Goulding, coauthor of *Changing Lives Through Redecision Therapy,* and cofounder of the Western Institute for Group and Family Therapy, for the use of Dorothy's case history.

DOROTHY *(to the empty chair)*: I don't want to see you because you've abused me all my life. You have a raging temper and no control.

THERAPIST: Say more.

DOROTHY: You've always hated me and blamed me. When I was a kid, you chased me around with a hairbrush or a knife. I was the oldest and you blamed me for everything the others did. You even beat me up and then would deny you did it and ask me how I got the bruises.

THERAPIST: Tell her, "You were crazy."

DOROTHY: You were out of control and I suppose you were psychotic.

THERAPIST: And where is your father when all this is going on?

DOROTHY: He traveled a lot because of his business, but he knew what went on. He was sympathetic and understanding. I don't know how I'd have survived without him.

THERAPIST: Pick a specific scene. When your mother is brutal and your father knows about it. Be there and tell it.

DOROTHY: One time she got terribly upset over something I'd written in school. She read into it some kind of insult to herself, I guess.

THERAPIST: Be there in the scene. Be an invisible presence and describe what you are seeing. Understand?

DOROTHY: Yes. The mother won't stop beating and screaming at the child, so the father phones the doctor to come and give the mother a sedative.

THERAPIST: So both the father and the doctor know this is a crazy, dangerous lady. What do they do for the little girl?

DOROTHY *(with surprise)*: Nothing. I always stay in my room when the doctor comes to the house.

THERAPIST: Who takes you to your room?

DOROTHY: I just go. Poor Dad, the last thing he needed was for people to know what went on in our house. It could have ruined his business. He always said, "What goes on under this roof never goes out the door."

THERAPIST: What else does he say?

DOROTHY: "Don't upset your mother. Do what she wants. Peace at any price."

THERAPIST: Good God! You say that as if it's okay.

(Therapist and Dorothy are silent.)

THERAPIST: Dorothy, leave this scene for just a moment. I want to ask you a question. Do you have children?

DOROTHY: Yes, a daughter.

THERAPIST: And do you treat her the way your mother treated you?

DOROTHY: No, never. I'd die first.

THERAPIST: Congratulations. You know, don't you, that lots of abused children grow up to be abusers. How old is your daughter?

DOROTHY: She's eight.

THERAPIST: Now, as an experiment, pretend your daughter is in the home where you grew up. Your mother is screaming and about to start beating her. What do you do?

DOROTHY: I'd stop that bitch if I had to kill her.

THERAPIST: Oh, so you don't hide your daughter in the bedroom so the doctor won't see her? You don't let the situation go on, knowing that every day your daughter is in danger?

(Dorothy shakes her head silently.)

THERAPIST: You would protect your daughter.

(Another silence.)

THERAPIST: Now, remove your daughter from this scene and be yourself, the little girl in the bedroom. You've been beaten. Your father comes in and says what?

DOROTHY: He says that I . . . that I have to stop crying so the doctor won't hear me. *(sobbing)* Oh, my God! How could you? Oh, Daddy, how could you? My mother was crazy and you didn't protect me. He abused me, too, by not protecting me. They were both abusers.

THERAPIST: That's right. And somehow you found the strength to survive well. Now, the important piece in all of this is simple. It's not whether you visit your mother, with or without guilt. The important part is whether you're still treating yourself the way your father treated you. For instance, do you take your daughter to the doctor but not take yourself? Do you feed your daughter appropriately and feed yourself inappropriately? Do you treat yourself as well as you treat your daughter? Do you give yourself the best possible love, care, and protection? Let's get to those issues next time you work in here.

Dorothy had finally recognized, after a lifetime of denial, that her father had not been her sympathetic fellow victim, deserving of protection and gratitude, but her exploiter and victimizer. A father like Dorothy's, or Gloria Steinem's, who in full consciousness and to suit his own convenience abandons his child to an abusive and possibly psychotic mother, is not merely an abandoning father. He is an abusive one.

What Makes Abuse Abuse?

So much has been written about child abuse. How could there be anything left to say? What can we add to the countless stories of children beaten, raped, exploited, humiliated, and even killed by parents, especially fathers, without merely going over familiar ground?

Perhaps what we can contribute is a clearer sense of what constitutes abuse. For all the examples in print, the term itself remains vague. Some writers focus on sensational but relatively rare behaviors, such as infant rape or ritual torture. Others discuss abuse in terms so broad that they could apply to almost any attempt at parental discipline or control. Where's the common denominator?

Is every child who has ever been spanked or yelled at or ignored an abused child? Or every child who ever overheard his parents making love? Surely not. Parents can't be expected to be perfect and children are not so fragile that anything less than A-plus parenting will destroy them. Also, a young child's needs are so insatiable that not even the finest parents in the world can hope to satisfy them all.

Abuse requires a consistent message to a child that the parent's gratifi-

cation is more important than the child's well-being, and that the child will be punished for any acts of self-assertion or self-protection.

Let's look at the key phrases in this definition.

A consistent message: Even the most loving parent is bound to be impatient or selfish once in a while. It's the dominant pattern of behavior that counts. It's true that highly destructive behaviors, such as rape or seduction or life-threatening violence, are abusive even if they happen only once. Realistically speaking, though, parents who do such things once are likely to do them more than once.

The parent's gratification: A parent who uses a child sexually obviously values his own gratification over the child's well-being. But, less obviously, so does the parent who takes out his temper on a child, or habitually puts her down or shoves her aside for fear of upsetting the other parent.

Abusive parents use children as involuntary partners in a psychodrama, targets for the parents' dark-side aspects of rage, violence, domination, cruelty, selfishness or lust. A child needs to be able to trust her parents' *intentions.* When a child understands, consciously or not, that she is being sacrificed, trust is destroyed.

Jenna and Machiko—Dinner-Table Conversation

Daughters are frequently sacrificed to their father's ill temper or impatience. Here are two stories of fathers who systematically made mealtime a hell for their small daughters, for no reason except their apparent pleasure in bullying the helpless.

Jenna, a young woman whom we interviewed, described dinnertime when she was a child. Her father, an athletic coach, sat at the table barking orders. Anything that wasn't done to his satisfaction was rewarded with a blow to the face or head. Jenna, customarily seated at her father's right, ended up sprawled on the floor at least once a night. Grown up, Jenna giggled as she described this brutal ritual, blaming herself for being "stupid enough to earn a couple of good ones" every night.

Machiko was a client whose current problems were rooted in

paternal abuse. During her first therapy session, when I asked what she wanted to change, she answered, "I want to learn to control my temper."

"Remember a recent scene where you lost your temper," I suggested, "and tell it first person, present tense, as if you are there now."

"I'm a flight attendent on a transpacific flight," she said, "working the first-class cabin during dinner. A passenger, an Asian man around fifty-five, calls me over. At first, I can't hear him over the engine noise. When I lean closer to catch what he's saying, he starts pinching my breast with his chopsticks. I go into a rage. I scream to the other passengers, 'Do you see what this man is doing to me?' And I shout at him, 'Who the hell do you think you are?'

"My supervisor, observing how I'm raving and ranting, believes I've lost control. She files a disciplinary report and I'm suspended for several months. I'm told my conduct has been totally unprofessional."

"Machiko," I said, "return in your imagination to a scene when you were much younger and someone treated you badly and you felt a similar rage. Tell it in the first person, present tense, as if you are there now."

"I am sitting with my six brothers and sisters at the dinner table with my parents. We're all eating with chopsticks. Since I'm only about three, I occasionally drop some food. Every time I do, my father raps my knuckles hard with his chopsticks. He really hurts me and I'm so angry and there's nothing I can do."

"Stay in this scene," I told her. "Look at your father sitting next to you and scream at him, "Who the hell do you think you are—hurting me with your chopsticks?"

Her face contorted with rage. "Who the hell do you think you are," she screamed, "hurting me with your chopsticks?"

"How are your father and the airline passenger alike?" I asked her.

"They hurt me with their chopsticks," she said.

"How are you different now than when you were that victimized little girl?"

"I'm an adult," she realized.

"As an adult, how might you respond to that passenger differently from the way you did?"

She calmed down. "Well, first I notice that he's not my father and I'm not a little girl." Her face lit up. "Ah!" she said, "I could go directly to my supervisor and tell her that the man in 2B is drunk and I need her help."

"Do you see yourself doing that next time you feel enraged?" I asked.

She nodded. "Yes."

"So what have you redecided?"

She took a deep breath. "It's okay to get angry but not to explode in a way that will penalize me. I rubber-banded to the past, but I don't have to do that. I can look for an effective rational response."

"Because this is not the past and the drunken passenger is not your father and you're not still a helpless little girl?"

Machiko nodded firmly in agreement.

Deflecting Anger

The emotional consequences of abuse are usually far more lasting than the physical damage. Bruises disappear but hurts to the self-concept can last a lifetime. Some victimized children, like Jenna, learn to deflect their anger from the abuser and onto themselves, taking the blame for the punishment. Others, like Machiko, may direct their anger, even years later, at anyone who reminds them of the abuser. Self-denigration and free-floating hostility are both harmful emotions to carry around, yet the child whose self-concept and well-being are under habitual attack is highly likely to develop one or both of them.

The Child's Well-being: How high does the child's well-being rank in the parents' priorities? A high-ranking child is cherished. A low-ranking child is abused. A father who fails to pay child support or who consistently misses visitations, or a mother who buys herself designer dresses but gets her daughter's clothes at garage sales, sends a message to the child that she doesn't matter. The common denominator is the parent's message that the child is to be sacrificed to the temper, pleasure, or convenience of others.

In hard times, parents may fail to provide even basic necessities yet still support a child's well-being. The classic Italian film *Two Women* takes place during World War II. A twelve-year-old girl and her youthful mother, played by Sophia Loren, wander the countryside as refugees. Constantly hungry, they share terrible dangers and are even gang-raped. Yet the girl overcomes the shock of her ordeal because she is supported by her mother's great love.

Even physical punishment is not always necessarily harmful. In the early days of their relationship, Annie Sullivan often had to wrestle little Helen Keller into submission, to calm her enough to teach her sign language. Yet once the blind-and-deaf Helen came to understand the great gift that "Teacher" was trying to give to her, she was filled with an immense and grateful love untainted by resentment; for there was no cruelty or self-serving behind Annie Sullivan's actions—only the determination to help an enraged and tragically isolated child to communicate.

The core issue, then, is whether the parent or parent-surrogate's actions are intended to support the child's growth, learning, well-being, and individual rights.

Punished for self-assertion or self-protection: Abusive parents deny their children rights as individuals. Like the torturers in George Orwell's *1984,* they soon learn what their children fear the most and use it against them. It doesn't matter whether the punishment is a beating or a threat of abandonment or silent sneers. As long as the purpose is to exercise domination by means of physical or mental pain, then it's abuse.

Maggie—Who Got the Message

High-strung, thirty-year-old Maggie had come into therapy in a fragile state. "I saw *La Traviata* last night and cried my eyes out," she said.

"What was happening?" I asked.

Her reply came in a flood. "The father was holding his son. Even though he had separated the son from the woman he loved, I still wept at the sight of such fatherly love. I wanted a father to take care of me like that. I wish somebody would, but I get scared any time a man gets too close. Yet I'm just as scared of having to take care of myself. I've had to be responsible all my life and I hate it."

"Imagine your father in that chair, Maggie," I said to her, motioning to an empty chair nearby. "Tell him what he taught you about being responsible."

She swallowed hard. "Dad, you taught me that being responsible is a terrible activity. I always had to baby-sit my sister who was handicapped and couldn't even feed herself or use a toilet. I had to clean your filthy bird cage too. I had to be nice to you even though you were mean to us. You gave our mother fifty dollars a week that had to buy everything for five people. You said you'd buy your own food, but then you'd take ours. We used the same worn-out towels and sheets for fifteen years. You locked up our toys. We had to break in and sneak them out, scared to death you'd catch us. You wouldn't pay for a pair of jeans so I could look like the other kids. I had to make my own clothes, while you traveled to Europe each year. After Mom made you move out, I had to clean a neighbor's toilets to make money for food. And the cotillion! Damn you, the cotillion! Mom knew you wouldn't want to spend money on a dress for me, so she hid the invitation. I went for years thinking there was something horribly wrong with me because everyone else got invited and I didn't."

She was silent for a long moment, so I asked, "How would he punish you?"

"In all sorts of ways," she said.

"Would you tell him about one time in particular?"

Her voice shook. "Dad, I *hated* that scene you made in the airport when we came back from visiting your family in France. That customs official asked if you had any liquor with you. You said no, and I asked, 'Dad, doesn't that box of chocolate-covered berries have liquor in it?' So you made me sit in front of the customs official and eat the whole box with you, just to avoid paying the duty. That was how you punished an eight-year-old for speaking up and being truthful."

"Did your father love you, Maggie?"

"In his way, yes, I'm sure he did."

If this was her experience of a man's "love," no wonder she was too "scared" to let a man "too close." We'll be dealing with how Maggie was able to revise her expectations in a later chapter.

Abuse and Power, Fathers and Daughters

Nonabusive fathers view themselves as mentors, not masters. They see their children as potential equals, temporarily under their protection. In contrast, the abusive parent sees the child as a permanent inferior.

One problem between fathers and daughters is that daughters, unlike sons, never do grow quite as big and strong and powerful as their fathers. This makes it harder for fathers to respect them and easier to abuse them.

Another cause of trouble is what the culture teaches men about women.

John Milton and the Daughters of Eve

John Milton, the English poet, is a hero of the democratic tradition. During the 1640s, he helped overthrow King Charles I and was active in the parliamentary government that followed. Over the next dozen years or so, he developed many of the crucial arguments behind our own Bill of Rights, such as a free press and the separation of Church and State. All this makes him one of the world's greatest champions of freedom.

For everyone but women.

In *Paradise Lost,* he retold the Garden of Eden story, elaborating on the wickedness of Eve—so easily seduced by Satan, so seductive toward Adam. Next, in *Samson Agonistes*, he retold another Biblical tale of female evil, of how the cunning Delilah tricked the infatuated Samson.

To him, the moral was plain: Women are wicked. Given the least power, they will use it to destroy men. Therefore, God has made men responsible for controlling women. The wise man will pay no attention to what they want, how they feel, or anything they say.

As the chorus sang in *Samson Agonistes:*

> Therefore God's universal law
> Gave to the man despotic power
> Over his female in due awe,
> Nor from that right to part an hour,
> Smile she or lour:
> So shall he least confusion draw
> On his whole life, not swayed
> By female usurpation, nor dismayed.

In the seventeenth century, this was actually quite a commonplace attitude. As Dr. Wolfgang Lederer explains in *The Fear of Women,* it goes back to the beginnings of the Judeo-Christian tradition. It also lasted a very long time. The great Russian novelist Leo Tolstoy, who lived well into the twentieth century, wrote this lecture to himself into his diary when he was nineteen years old:

> Regard the company of women as an unavoidable social evil and keep away from them as much as possible. Who indeed is the cause of sensuality, indulgence, frivolity and all sorts of other vices in us, if not women? Who is to blame for the loss of our natural qualities of courage, steadfastness, reasonableness, fairness, etc., if not women?[1]

How does a man who holds such views raise his daughters? We'll consider Leo Tolstoy later. For now, let's look at John Milton.

When his first wife left him within a year of their marriage, he promptly began to agitate for the legalization of divorce—for men only. He dropped the issue when his bride returned. Soon widowed, he married again and was widowed again.

Neither wife gave him a son, only daughters. What must have seemed like a trial sent by God turned out to be a great convenience. After the revolution to overthrow the monarchy failed, John Milton ended up poor, blind, and under virtual house arrest, dependent on his daughters for household and secretarial help. Day after day, year after year, they took dictation, proofread, and copied his enormous output. He taught them to read Latin aloud, but not to understand it, then required them to recite Latin works to him for several hours a day.

Not surprisingly, such a man's daughters got little thanks from their father for all these labors. Instead, he told the world that they were stupid, rebellious creatures incapable of appreciating their father's genius. And this is how they have been portrayed in literary histories and Milton biographies.

Like Kagekiyo, John Milton's last years were spent as an old, poor, blind survivor of a defeated cause. Kagekiyo used the experience to transcend his cultural conditioning and so became capable of loving and appreciating a daughter. Milton never did.

Nancy—Growing Up Sexy

The Milton family history exemplifies how a cultural contempt for women discouraged a seventeenth-century man from loving his own daughters. Nancy's father was a man of the twentieth century. Unlike John Milton, he was not the type to devote his life to a political cause, a religion, or an art. Unlike John Milton, he did not flee from sexuality but cultivated it.

Yet his ideas about women were no less oppressive.

Nancy was twenty-four when she came into therapy. A tall, long-legged redhead, she had a career to match her glamorous looks, as a booking agent for musical groups. Yet the first thing she said was "I feel totally out of control."

"Give an example," I suggested. "Use the present tense."

"Well, last week, a new client I'm with at work offers to drive me to the airport. Except, he takes me to a motel instead."

"Do you refuse to go in?"

"No. Actually, I'm thrilled that he wants me so much. I feel absolutely compelled to go to bed with him. But I end up missing my plane to New York and being late for my appointments the next day. And I feel guilty about that, and most of all I feel out of control."

"Will you pick a scene from an earlier time where you're learning about sex and men?" I asked.

She answered promptly. "I'm ten years old and I'm at the beach in L.A. with my dad. Every time a woman goes by, he analyzes her figure for me. When one of them has a particularly great body, he tells me, 'That's how I want you to look. That's how a girl's supposed to look. That's what men want.' I tell him to stop, that I feel embarrassed, but he insists, 'You're mine. I want to be proud of you.' "

"What was your father's relationship with your mother?"

"I know he saw other women because he used to tell me about it—how good they were in bed and what a man likes and doesn't like."

"Your mother knew what was going on?"

"Oh, yes. She hated it, but what could she do? She had lovers, too. She once told me, 'I do it because your father does. I refuse to sit around at home feeling sorry for myself.' "

Measures of Worth

Nancy's story demonstrates the overwhelming importance of attitude. Her father had never seduced or raped his daughter, yet he had abused her sexually and taught her to degrade herself.

By openly flaunting his affairs before his wife, he had taught his daughter that a woman's feelings don't matter. By defining female success as becoming "what men want," he trained her to view herself as a sex object. By telling her that she was *his* and should aim to do *him* proud, he denied her right to an individual identity.

John Milton saw women as instruments of Satan. Nancy's father saw them as sexual conveniences. Neither perceived them as fully human, and therefore neither could truly love a daughter. Unloved by her father, Nancy grew up not knowing how to love herself. She measured her worth by her desirability and put the sexual demands of the merest stranger ahead of her own career. How else should she feel but "out of control"?

Subpersonalities

It seems like such a puzzle. How can an avowed enemy of despotism, like John Milton, preach despotism toward women? How can a beautiful, successful woman like Nancy yield with the submissiveness of a slave to the demands of a stranger?

Actually, it's not all that puzzling. The human personality is a complex structure made up of many different behavior patterns. Usually, one personality pattern is dominant, but secondary patterns may take over consistently enough to function as distinct *subpersonalities.*

Subpersonalities are not multiple personalities of the *Three Faces of Eve* variety. They don't lead separate lives under separate names but are the different sides of a single identity. Yet subpersonalities can be so different from the dominant personality that people who know us in one context would hardly recognize us in another.

We may be efficient at work yet a frazzled wreck at home. We may be gloomy when sober yet lively when we drink. We may be sociable with strangers yet not have a thing to say to relatives. We may be indulgent with our children yet demanding with our lovers. We may be outgoing with men yet shy with women. We may be reserved in church yet wildly ecstatic in the bedroom. We may be any of these, or exactly the reverse.

Having such a repertory of behaviors is normal, as long as the behaviors are healthy. Our subpersonalities give us our adaptability. But they may also embody our inner conflicts.

Both our dominant personality and our subpersonalities originate in childhood, in response to formative experiences. In adulthood, subpersonalities are activated when some person or circumstance triggers unconscious memories of those experiences. If the formative experience was a damaging one and has not been resolved, then the subpersonality may be driven by a repetition compulsion.

Subpersonalities and Abuse

Most schools of psychology agree that abused children can go one of two ways. Either they identify themselves as victims and go through life choosing situations where they will be victimized, or else they identify with the aggressor and learn to victimize others.

Victims victimize to play out incomplete scenarios. Children who live with physical abuse spend much of their time in fear and pain and anger, yearning to fight back but knowing they lack the strength. In later years, when such feelings arise again, they may look around to act out their rage on someone "safe." In the grip of the subpersonality that developed in response to the original abuse, the grown-up victim may attack his own child as if that child were the person who originally attacked him.

The Victim-Rescuer-Persecutor Subpersonalities

Because the abusing parent is in the grip of a repetition compulsion, he usually feels helpless to stop. Back in his abused childhood, he solemnly swore never to treat a child of his own that way, and now he's doing it. To avoid the shame and guilt, he may then blame the child. Like John Milton, he may see himself as his victim's victim.

This is easy to do because many people who grow up abused are used to experiencing a triad of roles. One role is that of *victim*, the target of the abuse. The second is *rescuer*, the one who protects. The third is *persecutor*, the one who abuses others. In many families, members constantly trade these roles. Psychiatrist Stephen Karpman calls this pattern the *Drama Triangle*.[2]

As roles get traded, each individual keeps shifting from one position to another. A teenaged boy, for example, is beaten by his drunken father, making him a victim. The next moment, he runs to protect his mother or a younger child, making him a rescuer. Then he turns on his father in a rage, hurling insults and missiles, behaving like a persecutor. All this may take place in a matter of minutes, even seconds, the characteristic feelings of all three modes experienced in rapid succession.

In manhood, this same boy may be unable to separate such feelings, habitually shifting from frustration and helplessness to defiance and moral indignation to rage and vindictiveness, with no real awareness of what is happening or why.

Abusers of both sexes are far more likely to see themselves as victims or rescuers than as persecutors. Witch hunters burning "witches," Ku Klux Klansmen lynching African-Americans, and Nazis driving Jews into gas chambers all claimed to feel threatened by their victims and to be protecting society. The same thing happens within the family. Joel Steinberg, the attorney who beat his adopted six-year-old daughter to death, claimed that he had acted to defend himself and others against Lisa's evil psychic powers.

The tendency of abusers to blame the victim is partly a matter of *projection*, our wish to assign our own unacceptable feelings to the other person. "You hate me," the parent screams, when it may be the parent who, like Dorothy's mother, hates the child. But blaming the victim also comes from the way we confuse our *victim, rescuer,* and *persecutor* roles.

The Multiplication of Abuse

When a parent blames the abuse on the child, the abuse is multiplied. Most children will accept the blame and turn it on themselves. Because girls as a group are less esteemed by society, the self-worth of an abused daughter is particularly vulnerable. "If I were any good," she thinks, "they'd love me and not treat me this way."

Dorothy, the woman whose father had hidden her from the doctor after her beatings, put it this way: "I grew up absolutely convinced that there are two kinds of people, those who get catered to and those who have to cater. It was my hard luck that I was one of those who have to cater. I was convinced that you were born one way or the other and that nothing could change it, that it was your fate or your genes and you had to live with it. I believed in my heart that I could never really be loved and that I would have to earn my right to exist by being useful and pleasing the powerful."

Daddy is the earliest symbol of the male sex for a little girl. When she grows up, all other men partake to some extent of her father. Any man who strongly impinges on a woman's life, either as an authority figure or an object of love, is bound to activate something of what she felt for him. If he had taught her to be a victim, she may tend to be drawn to victimizing men.

A Father-Daughter-Lover Triangle

Somehow, Claire had prevailed upon her father, Joe, to come in for a trial session of family therapy. Claire was in her late twenties, small and plump, with a sweet but anxious face framed by dark, curly hair. Joe was a strong, fit man in his early fifties, dressed in an expensive business suit, with a look of supreme annoyance.

I invited them to come in and sit down, then asked Joe to speak first. After more than half an hour, Claire asked if she could say something.

"You'll wait till I'm finished!" Joe snapped at her.

I attempted to intervene. "Joe, will you give Claire a chance to speak?"

Joe snapped at me. "I'll speak till I'm finished or I'm walking out."

When I insisted, he did walk out. Claire started to rise, then settled back in her chair. I asked her, "Has he ever walked out like this before?"

"All the time," she said.

"What do you usually do?"

"Run after him and apologize and give up on what I want."

"Why didn't you this time?"

"Because I'm here and you're here, and maybe there's a way out."

"Are you willing to divorce your dad?" I asked.

The idea took her by surprise but raised a smile. I had an idea that she would make rapid progress, and she did.

Claire's usual response, to beg for favors and apologize when refused, betrayed a habit of defeat that Joe's treatment had drilled into her. But Joe was not the only man who could activate this mode in Claire.

Three months into her therapy, Claire met Edward, formerly an army officer, now a computer consultant living in Silicon Valley. Edward set about taking over Claire's life as thoroughly as her father had ever done, and Claire yielded in a state of mixed resentment and relief.

They were to be married in Boston, where his family lived. Edward flew on ahead to arrange the wedding, and Claire followed a week later, carrying along a wedding gown hastily concocted by a seamstress friend. It wasn't until she had been in Boston for a day or two that she realized what she was getting into. Edward bossed his mother around and she scurried to meet his endless demands in an all-too-familiar pattern. Fortunately, Claire had learned about the repetition compulsion in therapy. Recognizing the pattern, she called off the wedding.

The Perpetuation of Abuse

The greatest problem facing the abused daughter is the lasting effect on the self-concept and the way the repetition compulsion assures that she will keep encountering the same painful set of circumstances throughout life.

Greta's father was a grimly stubborn man, an immigrant from Eastern Europe, whose word was law and who refused to allow Greta to have any impact. Once he said *no* to something, it didn't matter whether she politely asked, patiently reasoned, and calmly explained, or if she pleaded, wept, begged, demanded, groveled, or threatened to run away and kill herself. Her father's *no* was *no*.

To get away from home, Greta eloped at sixteen, but she soon found that she had married an older man who treated her much as her father had done. Eventually her husband died and she remarried, only to find herself in the same predicament. Greta concluded that there must be something innately wrong with her if men treated her this way. It was her fault. She deserved it.

In actuality, there *was* something wrong. In part, it was her choice of extremely patriarchal men. In part, it was her way of meeting the situation. At the prospect of yet another defeat coming, Greta would get so angry and frustrated that she would fall apart and lose control. This made it easy for her husbands to see her as an unreasonable being who was not worth listening to. But Greta hadn't been born this way. It was something she had learned from coming up again and again against the stone wall of her father's cruel resistance.

The Nonrecognition of Abuse

Today, we are shocked at the rude way that Joe shut Claire up, or the brute obstinacy of Greta's father. Yet, not so long ago, people would have been just as shocked at Claire for interrupting or at Greta for arguing. In many cultures, to this day, a daughter is expected to defer to her father no matter what, to start learning early that her role in life is to serve and obey.

The very concept of daughter abuse is new. As late as the 1940s, many little Chinese girls were still having their feet bound, a crippling procedure that meant deforming or dislocating every bone in the foot. To this day, in parts of East Africa and the Moslem world, prepubescent little girls have the clitoris and sometimes the labia surgically removed. The wealthiest may have it done in a hospital under anesthesia, but most must be held down screaming by three or four adult women while a midwife goes to work with a razor blade.[3]

These are cruel and painful things to describe, but the treatment of women has often been cruel and painful. Where such practices are the custom, people accept them as normal. Foot binding and clitoridectomy are considered necessary to make girls acceptable as wives. A wife with no clitoris won't have much desire to be unfaithful, and a wife who can hardly walk won't have much opportunity. Besides, men taught to admire scarred genitals and atrophied feet find natural ones repulsive. In our own society, where we are taught to see anorexic models as beautiful, many men reject normal women as "fat."

In many societies, the unmarried daughter who loses her virginity is thought to have disgraced her father and is thrown out of the house—thus ensuring a steady supply of prostitutes. The Bible calls for an unchaste daughter to be publicly stoned to death. This occurs in Garcia Lorca's play *The House of Bernarda Alba,* set in Spain in the 1930s. In some times and places, victims of rape have either been killed or ordered to commit suicide. Until 1870, in California, it was legal for a man to beat his wife or daughter, so long as the stick he used was no thicker than his thumb.

We think of our own society as cruel and violent, but in many ways things have actually gotten much better. At least in some quarters, women have substantial recognition by at least some men as *like subjects* rather than merely *love objects*—that is, as fellow human beings. At least we now see abuse as abuse, not as appropriate behavior.

The Discovery of Abuse

As democratic ideas became dominant during the nineteenth century, the abuse of women and children first came to be recognized as a problem. The novels of Charles Dickens were crucial to this change. Dickens was the first major author to build his stories around victimized children—defenseless little outcasts, suffering horrors at the hands of parents and society. Dickens himself had been such a child, and he portrayed his boyhood experience through such characters as David Copperfield and Oliver Twist. Many of his suffering children were also little girls, however, whom he idealized even more than he idealized the boys.

Charles Dickens's novels were to child abuse what Harriet Beecher Stowe's *Uncle Tom's Cabin* was to slavery. Dickens and Stowe changed the nineteenth-century world by turning traditional values upside down. Suddenly, the poor and despised were presented as saints and the high and mighty looked like fools or villains. By mixing sentiment and drama with allusions to the Bible, Dickens and Stowe reminded the public that the weak and helpless are to be loved and protected, not victimized.

The Daughter as Innocent Victim

Dickens and Stowe won sympathy for social victims by making them defenseless, harmless, and forgiving. This was achieved by idealization. Stowe's Uncle Tom is a saint and martyr. So is Dickens's Florence Dombey. They are pure victim, sometimes mixed with rescuer, but without a grain of vengeful persecutor in their nature. It's easy to see why the authors found it necessary to present them that way. There was an ingrained public perception of both blacks and women as subhuman and dangerous. If flaws had been shown in Uncle Tom or Florence, many readers would have lost all sympathy.

Besides, for a very long time, women had been seen in either-or terms: all good or else all bad, a madonna or else a whore. This point of view continues to have power. During the first quarter of the twentieth century, the tremendously popular silent films of D. W. Griffith perpetuated the image of the pure and innocent female victim, especially the pure and innocent daughter.

Nothing inspired Griffith more than the abuse of young girls by their fathers. The silent movie *Broken Blossoms* featured perhaps the most appalling scene of parental violence ever filmed. A girl of about twelve, played by the angelic Lillian Gish, locks herself in a closet to hide from her drunken prize fighter father. As the brute starts smashing in the door, she begins to scurry like a trapped rat, screaming and beating the walls in mad terror. A few years later, in *Way Down East,* the same angel-faced actress played a teen who is seduced and abandoned. Her father does the traditional thing and throws her out to die.

In Griffith's abusive father-daughter situations, the father is the villain, the daughter his saintly victim. Plainly, by the 1920s, a popular artist like Griffith could rely on the public to be horrified by the spectacle of paternal abuse.

The change since Milton's time had been revolutionary. The bullying male was no longer God's animal trainer, struggling to control a dangerous female beast. Instead, *he* was the beast, exploiting his brute strength to harm a defenseless angel.

Since Griffith's day, there has been yet another revolution. Sometime during the 1960s, the passive Dickens-Stowe-Griffith heroine went out of style. Today, we are often impatient with weak, submissive victims. We expect the abused to stand up and fight or else get out.

Yet there is something so deep in a child's need for a parent's love that it will keep even the adult child in an abusive situation, hoping that things will get better. It can be the same for boys as girls, so it has nothing to do with the masochism traditionally attributed to women. In a recent radio interview, former light-heavyweight boxing champion Donny LaLonde described fighting his way to the top in hopes of winning the approval of the stepfather he described as alcoholic and neglectful. An eloquent spokesman for the child-protection movement, Donny emphasized that a small child's need for parental love is so powerful that he or she will pay almost any price for even a little bit. Growing up means finding better ways to satisfy those early unmet needs.

4

THE PAMPERING FATHER AND HIS SPOILED DAUGHTER

◆

He who binds to himself a joy
Doth the winged life destroy.

—William Blake
fragment from the *Rossetti Manuscript*

The Promise

There's an old Jewish joke about a newly wealthy family arriving at an expensive resort hotel with the daughter in a wheelchair. The desk clerk says to the father, "What a pity about your little girl, that she can't walk." To which the father proudly replies, "Don't worry, she can walk all right. But, thank God, she doesn't have to."

That's what spoiling is all about.

The pampering father makes his daughter an implicit promise: that she will never have to take care of herself because the world will take care of her. The key to the spoiled daughter's character is her sense of entitlement. She grows up believing that the world is obliged to live up to her father's promise.

The spoiled daughter lives in a fairy-tale world where all stories are supposed to end happily, at least for her. Wanting to live in such a world is not unique to the spoiled daughter. What sets her apart is her conviction that she has a *right* to happy endings—and happy middles and beginnings, too. Others may have to struggle for what they need or want, but she is exempt from the human condition.

Blind Love

To a neglected or ill-treated daughter, the pampering father may look like an ideal parent. To the sort of father who can't relate to a daughter, he may seem in possession of some mysterious skill. Yet the pampering father can hurt his daughter as badly as any distant or abusive father.

It's sometimes surprising who turns out to be a pamperer. Some swaggering tough guy, who ordinarily scorns women and hates any appearance of weakness, may carry on like a besotted fool over a daughter, especially an only daughter. She is, after all, *his,* an extension of himself, which sets her apart from the ordinary females sired by other men.

Some will pamper a daughter as a way of pampering the hidden feminine side of themselves. Some will pamper her because they're too competitive to pamper a son. As one interviewee expressed it, having a daughter gave him "a safe place to be tender."

Some will pamper a daughter because it's less dangerous than pampering her mother. A little girl, after all, lacks a woman's weapons. A woman can leave a man, divorce him, have affairs, call in the police, even shoot him dead. Or she may do none of these things yet still crush him with a word or a look. But a small daughter is disarming because she is disarmed. Her father can feel all-powerful before her, like a god.

If he chooses to be a stern or cruel god, a father will be feared. But if he becomes an indulgent, giving god, he will be adored. How else, except through a daughter, can the ordinary human joe experience adoration? His wife knows too much about him. His sons try to match themselves against him. But an idolized daughter will sometimes idolize her father all the days of her life.

Of course, not every pamperer spoils his daughter for deep, dark reasons. Sometimes, like Billy Bigelow, he's simply picked up the message that it's the right thing to do. Or perhaps he's come to fatherhood late, when other men his age are already grandfathers, and the experience overwhelms him. One post-fiftyish first-time father, Warren Beatty, put it this way:

> It's the biggest experience I ever had . . . the zenith of exis-
> tence. It was a matter of great pride to me that she knew my
> voice as soon as she entered the world.[1]

When a man feels that way about a child, it seems likely that he will pamper her.

From "I Need You" to "You Owe Me"

Ironically, most spoiled daughters don't feel spoiled at all. On the contrary, they may feel deprived and abused.

The spoiled daughter feels deprived because, like the little girl in the wheelchair joke, she has been trained to helplessness. She feels abused because she expects to be served, and that doesn't always happen. And so she feels ineffectual and frustrated, a humiliating condition that creates panic and rage. Her feeling toward others quickly escalates from *I need you* to *You owe me.*

Some spoiled daughters become *spoiled darlings,* successfully manipulating the daddies they depend on, and later the husbands. Others become *spoiled brats,* using tantrums when manipulation fails. It takes a very rare spoiled daughter to recognize her spoiled condition and make a conscious decision to grow up.

Babes in Toyland

Henrik Ibsen's famous play *A Doll's House* tells the story of a spoiled daughter who does make that decision. As a child, Nora's role in life was to agree with her father's opinions and be fun for him to play with. As a woman, her role is to agree with her husband's opinions and be fun for *him* to play with. A typical upper-middle-class Victorian woman, she goes directly from being her father's plaything to her husband's plaything, with no idea that anything else is possible for a woman. She is a doll, a toy, a pampered pet, but not a person.

Nora's story exemplifies the degrading effects of such a life. Not only must she beg and wheedle like a puppy to get favors from her provider-husband, but she hasn't a clue how to behave when action is required. A day comes when her father is dying and her husband is critically ill and she must have money to save her husband's life. To get it, she forges her father's name as cosigner on a loan, without the least awareness that she is risking blackmail and prison.

Nora is so well-meaning a character that it seems harsh to call her spoiled. Yet spoiled she is. If she had forged her father's name with some awareness of the risks, that would have been heroic. But she was quite unaware of the danger, because, in her dollhouse world, *of course* she had a right to what she needed and *of course* nothing really bad could ever happen. Later, when threatened with exposure, she counts on her husband, Torvald, to come dashing to her rescue like some storybook prince and is totally shocked when he displays self-centered anger instead.

As a character, Nora is more ideal than real. Another spoiled daughter might also have walked out on Torvald—in a rage over his failure to rescue her. But Nora is not angry so much as amazed—stunned that life and people should be so different from the way she had imagined. Shocked out of her spoiled daughter's illusions, she leaves her doll's house because she wants to grow up and start living in the real world.

This is the step that very few real-life spoiled daughters are willing to take. Spoiled daughters generally cling to their sense of entitlement *because* they're spoiled. It's a vicious circle. As long as a spoiled daughter keeps her sense of entitlement, she may spend

much of her life in anger and frustration, rightly feeling abused—
but for the wrong reasons.

A Dance of Death—Rhett and Bonnie

The spoiled daughter is programmed for disaster. Waltzing into
view we now see a familiar couple—Rhett Butler and his daughter,
Bonnie, from *Gone With the Wind*.

Rhett in his bachelor days was a dashing figure, a charming if
rapacious robber baron, cheerfully building a personal empire on
the ruin of the South in the Civil War. Unfortunately, he falls in
love with the even more rapacious Scarlett O'Hara, who loves
another man but marries Rhett for his money. After Bonnie is
born, Scarlett refuses to have sex with him anymore, so Rhett turns
to Bonnie for consolation.

Rhett is quite frank about what Bonnie means to him. He pretends to himself that she is her mother, Scarlett. In other words, he
uses his daughter as a surrogate for the wife who has rejected him.
Rhett can't say no to *"my* Bonnie." Rather than risk her rejection,
he yields to her every demand, whether it's not having her hair
combed, or eating off his plate, or sipping wine every night from
his glass.

When she is two, Rhett moves Bonnie's bed from the nursery to
his own room. When she is three, he starts taking her on trips.
When she is four, he buys her a pony and teaches her to jump.
When she wants him to raise the bar, he refuses because he knows
the pony's legs are too short. But Bonnie stamps her pretty little
foot, so Rhett gives in. The pony balks and Bonnie is thrown and
killed.

And what if Bonnie had not died at four? Well, what becomes of
little girls whose heavy-drinking fathers start them off on nightly
wine before they're two? What happens to little girls whose sexually
frustrated fathers sleep in the same room? What happens to little
girls whose fathers pretend to themselves that the daughter is the
wife?

The Incest Waltz—Nicole and Her Daddy

In F. Scott Fitzgerald's *Tender Is the Night,* the pampering father is, like Rhett, a handsome, virile, semiretired tycoon, with lots of time on his hands. After his wife's death, he turns for affection to his little daughter, Nicole. He takes her traveling and often cuddles with her in bed. Everyone is charmed by their mutual adoration. They are "just like lovers," people say.

Then, one day, they really *are* lovers. Nicole disintegrates and has to be institutionalized at fifteen. She makes a partial recovery, thanks to her psychiatrist, Dick Diver, whom she marries at eighteen, after which she never sees her father again. For the next dozen years, Dick sacrifices his career to Nicole's recurrent breakdowns. In the end, thanks to his full-time services, she makes a complete recovery. Not needing a psychiatrist anymore, she abandons him for a more glamorous man—a handsome, virile, ruthless man, rather like her father.

Thanks to her spoiling, Fitzgerald's Nicole is both victim and victimizer. Her role as the petted surrogate for her mother exposes her to the trauma of incest, but at the same time it trains her to believe that she is entitled to anything she wants, and that other people can be used and discarded. If we want to imagine Nicole's early childhood, we have only to read about Rhett and Bonnie. If we want to imagine Bonnie surviving her fall and growing up, we have only to look at Nicole.

Like Father, Like Husband—Jackie and the Two Jacks

Not all spoiled daughters end up in bed with their fathers. But many do end up in bed with facsimiles thereof.

In *The Kennedys,* a history of the President's family, Peter Collier and David Horowitz describe Jacqueline Kennedy's relationship with her father, Jack Bouvier, nicknamed "Black Jack."[2] Black Jack had the reputation of being one of the great womanizers of his day. Jackie looked like him, had been named for him, and was treated like a favorite child.

Her parents separated when she was eight. Jackie remained very close to her father and blamed her mother for the divorce. According to a boarding school classmate quoted by Collier and Horowitz, she would boast excitedly about her father's many sexual adventures, and scoff at her mother's distress over his infidelity. Her stories so glamorized her father that her friends would rush out to stare at him whenever he'd come to take her away for the weekend.

Jackie was attracted to Jack Kennedy from their first meeting. She was aware of his reputation for philandering but that may have been part of the appeal. Collier and Horowitz quote Chuck Spalding, a family friend of the Kennedys, who said that Jackie did not find men attractive unless they shared Black Jack's dangerous aura.

Jackie introduced Father Jack to Lover Jack, and they instantly recognized each other as kindred spirits. Their subjects of conversation were politics, sports, and women—the normal interests of "red-blooded men," according to Jackie.

Generalizing from her father's behavior, Jackie openly stated to friends that all men are unfaithful. Even so, she apparently found her own husband's infidelity hard to take. From the earliest days of their marriage, say Collier and Horowitz, Jack would abandon her at parties to sneak off with other women. He even kept a special "hideout" in Washington for sexual fun and games. Yet, for all his adventures, it was clear that Jack reserved for her a special place in his affections. Just as her father had done, he saw her as unique and set apart from other women.

So, despite her pain, Jackie stuck by her dynamic, charismatic husband. Apparently, growing up with a philandering father who treated her as uniquely precious had given her whatever it takes to cope with a philandering husband.

The Not-Quite-Human Sex

Pampering fathers feel free to spoil their daughters, as they would never spoil their sons, because daughters belong to the not-quite-human sex. To put it more bluntly, such fathers pet daughters because they see them more as pets than as people. They understand that sons must grow up, learn responsibility and competence, and become adults. But they don't see their daughters as ever becoming adults—merely women.

It's not that pampering fathers despise women; in societies where women are thoroughly despised and treated as chattel, spoiling is probably rare. A pampering father adores his daughter, and people must have status to be adored. Yet those we adore we never perceive as entirely human. To see someone as special, set apart, unlike others, is a denial of that person's humanity.

Turning Against an Indulged Daughter

The pampering father and spoiled daughter idolize each other. Almost inevitably, idols must fall. When a father "fails" his spoiled daughter, she may well rebel against him. When she "fails" him, he may turn openly abusive.

An idolized daughter may "fail" her father in any number of ways. She may turn out plain or pimpled or awkward, or too tall or short or fat or thin. She may resemble the mother her father still fears or the wife he resents. If he was counting on her to do him proud or to be his ideal companion, he may feel betrayed.

She may also turn out socially inept. Spoiled daughters are often unpopular. Frequently demanding their own way, they tend to alienate others. Or they may become charming but manipulative. The father does not realize that he has encouraged his daughter's less attractive tendencies. Instead, he blames her.

Some previously indulgent fathers will turn on a daughter as soon as she manifests a mind of her own. In traditional literature, the quarrel is usually over the daughter's marriage. Either the father selects a husband whom the daughter can't stand, or the daughter wants to choose for herself. In either case, the father's former love suddenly turns to rage.

In Samuel Richardson's *Clarissa*, the title character is tormented for not accepting her father's choice. In Henry Fielding's *Tom Jones*, Sophie is locked up for refusing to marry Blifil. In Henry

James's *Portrait of a Lady,* Gilbert Osmond threatens his daughter Pansy with the convent unless she forgets her sweetheart and marries a nobleman. This same theme appears again and again in Shakespeare. In *Romeo and Juliet,* Juliet must poison herself to avoid marrying Paris. In *Othello,* Desdemona's father disowns her for eloping with Othello. In *Much Ado about Nothing,* Hero's father publicly repudiates her over a baseless rumor that she has lost her virginity.

In most of these stories, the persecuted daughter is her father's *only child,* the apple of his eye, the person he claims to treasure most. Yet, when forced to choose between his own pride and her happiness, he chooses his pride. His behavior seems senseless until we look past his actions to his feelings. Then we can see that he is taking revenge on her, for preferring some other man over himself.

It's not that these fathers don't want their daughters to marry. They want them married, all right, but not to men they love. When the daughter dares to have a preference, the father reacts like a betrayed husband. Desdemona's father is quite explicit about it. He spitefully warns Othello, "Look to her, Moor, if thou hast eyes to see. She hath betray'd her father, and may thee."

In *King Lear,* Cordelia is not her father's only child, but she is far and away his favorite. Although she is about to be married, Lear commands her to swear that she loves no man but himself. When she says she will divide her love equally between father and husband, he disowns her.

Paternal behavior like this is emotionally incestuous. The daughter is a love object, not a like subject, a possession, not a person. The father attempts to control her for his own benefit, not hers. He stands firmly opposed to her having either feelings or a will of her own. Such behavior constitutes abuse.

Can't Buy Me Love

The daughter who is indulged in the midst of a chaotic family situation, or by a father with a hidden agenda, is put under a severe strain. She becomes spoiled in that she comes to feel entitled to being cared for and getting her own way. At the same time, she may be full of rage toward her father, because what he gives her doesn't make her happy. She may even feel guilty over being treated better than her mother or siblings. If her resentment surfaces, her father will see her as ungrateful, and she may even see herself that way. Or else, she may avoid her discomfort by denigrating his gifts, turning herself into the sort of person who takes what she can and repays it with hostility.

This situation often originates with a father in desperate need of the daughter's love. His pampering of the child then puts the mother on the spot. She gets to discipline the daughter while the father gets to indulge her. She gets to say *no* while the father says *yes*. If the father is hostile toward the mother, he may use this dynamic to forge an alliance between himself and the daughter against her. The mother can then counterattack by encouraging the child to believe that the father's gifts are no more than the daughter's due. At this point, the whole family is on a downward spiral.

Parents as Rivals for the Child

Ted grew up the younger of two sons in a family so distracted by parental quarrels that the children got scant attention. Ted became a man with a tremendous yearning for love but little trust in people, which made it difficult for him to relate to adults.

At twenty-six, he married Kate, a fellow high-school teacher. Kate was much like Ted's mother, rigid and bossy, with little affection to give. Two years later, Ellen was born, with Ted present at the birth. From the first instant, Ted was overwhelmed by the urge to protect and treasure this vulnerable little creature. Unconsciously, he saw a chance to relive his childhood through his daughter, and this time to make everything right.

Kate only wanted one child. Ted had hoped for more but now changed his mind. A second child would be an intruder, taking time, attention, and material resources away from precious Ellen.

Ellen became everything to Ted. He began to see Kate not as his partner in parenthood but as his rival. In the ensuing struggle, he learned to use Kate's rules and regulations against her. Kate, for example, had a rule against eating anything but fresh fruit between meals. When Ted took Ellen out, he would woo her with candy or ice cream, saying "This is our secret, okay, sweetheart? We won't tell Mommy because she'd get mad."

Ted and Kate fought over the control of Ellen, dividing on such issues as *nursery school* v. *a housekeeper, religious private school* v. *secular, day camp* v. *overnight.* Ellen grew up with two points clearly impressed on her mind: 1) that her future was the most important matter on earth, and 2) that her own wishes would not be heard. In short, thanks to the repetition compulsion and the generational nature of family conflict, Ted's child was suffering much the same childhood as Ted had endured.

When Ellen was nine, Ted and Kate divorced. Both sued for custody, but the judge made a division, giving Ellen to Kate during the week and to Ted on the weekends. Ted filled his lonely evenings by moonlighting as an insurance salesman, putting the extra money into Ellen's college fund.

Ellen no longer had to sit through her parents' fights, but now she was stuck with hearing her mother badmouth her father all week and her father badmouth her mother all weekend. In a way this was even worse, because it was harder to escape. Ellen's time with Ted was especially intense, because it was on the weekend and they were together almost continuously.

Meanwhile, his gifts kept coming—trips to Hawaii and Disneyland. He also kept paying for Ellen's orthodontia, her private school, and her summer camp, aside from the court-ordered support. It was easier for Ellen to accept her mother's word that Ted owed her all these things than to endure what would otherwise have been a sense of overwhelming obligation.

In her last year of high school, the California-bred Ellen applied to several Ivy League colleges and was accepted at Brown. From the day she stepped on board the plane, Ellen ceased all communication with her father and rationed her mother to one post card once a month.

After three months of agony, Ted flew to Providence. Ellen reluctantly agreed to meet him in a campus coffee shop. There, she coldly announced that she did not want him in her life, now or ever.

In tears, he reminded her of all he had done, all he had given.

"I was your child," she rejoined. "It was your job to support me. You can't use that as emotional blackmail against me now."

He was appalled. "Blackmail? I did it for love."

"You did it to *buy* love," she told him.

Roots and Wings

Young children feel most secure when raised with firm limits and clear rules. Traditionally, these have been paternal values, the gift of the father, and these are precisely what the spoiling father fails to provide. It's the task of the teenager to "break up the family," that is, to find enough fault with life at home to justify leaving and establishing a separate identity. Part of this process consists of transforming the father from a *love object* to a *like subject*, from an object of idealization to a human being. If a daughter fails to do this, she will either go on adoring and depending on him in a blind, childish way, or else—like Ellen—she'll come to hate him for his faults and go too far in separating.

As human beings, we all need wings, the ability to fly on our own. But we also need roots, a place of return. During the teen years, we grow our wings and experiment with their use, but that does not mean we have to give up our roots. Ellen at eighteen was in a more difficult situation than even she realized. She had cut away her roots, both in the physical meaning of a home and in the spiritual meaning of having people she belonged to. The fact that she was so spoiled in a material way could only add to her difficulties.

Separation is one thing and repudiation is another. If adolescent rebellion goes too fast or too far, if the home and father are destroyed instead of transformed and outgrown, the adolescent graduates not into healthy adulthood but into chaos. And, for most of us, chaos is too terrifying to live with.

Escape from Chaos

Spoiled daughters in their early teens often demand freedoms that they don't really want, in the unconscious expectation that their fathers will forbid it. But what happens if the father grants permission instead, and the daughter is left to deal with experiences she is not ready to handle?

Dave, a divorced father with custody of his fifteen-year-old Debbie, frequently brought women home overnight. So when Debbie asked if she and her boyfriend, Charlie, could use her bed for sex, Dave would have felt like a hypocrite refusing. As long as she was properly advised about safe sex, what was the problem?

So, at fifteen, Debbie began to spend her dates in bed instead of going out. After the novelty wore off, she got bored and broke up with Charlie. Almost immediately, she got into the same sort of relationship with Rick. Then he broke up with her. After that, she met Paul, who was having troubles with drugs and with his parents. Paul soon moved in with Dave and Debbie, bringing his troubles with him. By now, Debbie was so engulfed in her daily soap opera that she had no attention to spare for school, reading, or simply having youthful fun. And, much to Dave's amazement, she seemed angry with *him* about it.

Thanks to her father's indulgence, Debbie had been thrown into relationships that were too much for her. She may have been physically "ready" for sex, but she was hardly mature enough emotionally for a live-in relationship, especially with someone as troubled as Paul. Having given his permission, however, Dave felt disqualified from retracting it. Instead, he left Debbie's life up to Debbie, as if she were an adult, rather than an adolescent still in need of guidance.

Over the next few years, Debbie's life grew more and more

chaotic. Then, to Dave's utter astonishment, she quit college in the middle of her sophomore year to join a super-Orthodox Jewish community run by a gurulike *tsaddik*. All of a sudden, this liberated young woman was keeping a *kosher* kitchen, observing sabbath regulations, covering her head, wearing no makeup, and deferring to men.

Dave was a modern, secular, nonobservant Jew. It was beyond him how any daughter of his could choose such an archaic life-style. But Debbie found the change a vast relief. With her conversion and a visit to the ritual bath, she became a kind of born-again virgin. A marriage was arranged for her by a matchmaker. The rules of the community made life simple. If she had problems, she could take them to the *tsaddik*, who would tell her what to do. For Debbie, given too much freedom too early, the only freedom she had come to value was the freedom not to be free.

Spoiled Daughters from Another World

In the eleventh century, in Japan, a court lady called Murasaki wrote a meticulously detailed novel describing life among the beautiful people of the day. Longer than *War and Peace, The Tale of Genji* covers the better part of a century and features more than a hundred and fifty characters.[3] Many of these are pampering fathers and spoiled daughters.

Japan at the time was definitely on its way to becoming a patriarchal, Confucianist society. Political power was entirely in male hands and polygamy was well established. In the twelfth century, a revolution on the part of the military class would complete the transformation to patriarchy, establishing the foundations of the Japan we know today. In Murasaki's time, however, life among the ruling classes was still somewhat influenced by customs and attitudes inherited from the matriarchal past.

It was an age of revered female priestesses, healers, and shamans, as well as poets, novelists, and chroniclers, many of whom chose not to marry, although some had lovers. Women were carefully educated, and artistic talent and a fluent wit were considered sexually attractive, although serious scholarship was not. Women also retained control over their personal fortunes, even if they married. Men and women were both free to initiate courtships, either party wooing the other with love letters, poetry, flowers, perfume, works of art, or fine fabrics. Some matches were arranged, but others were begun and ended by mutual consent. Unmarried girls invited their lovers into their bedrooms at night as a matter of course. Married women occasionally had lovers also; although this was considered immoral, they were not punished if discovered and the children of adultery carried little stigma. Married daughters often lived on with their parents for years, until it was clear that the relationship was going to work. Sons-in-law had to defer to their wives' parents, but women had virtually no contact with their husbands' families.

Under such circumstances, the daughters of prominent families tended to be very well treated indeed. Never once, anywhere, in *The Tale of Genji,* does a man strike a woman. In the single case where a woman is threatened with physical violence, the man is portrayed as an outlandish barbarian.

The critical factor was that a daughter could often do more for her family than a son could do. If she married "up," her family rose with her, since her husband had to behave like a son to her parents. The father of an empress, for example, usually became the equivalent of prime minister. Little wonder, then, that fathers took a great interest in their daughters, especially if they promised to be bright and attractive. Daughters of the highest rank, therefore, were overwhelmingly indulged.

Genji, the charming, self-indulgent hero of the novel, has one son and one daughter. He tries to pay attention to his son, but his heart isn't in it. Dutifully, he sees to the boy's education and attempts to strengthen his character by making him work hard and giving him few rewards. As a result, the son becomes a serious-minded, successful man who hates his father.

Genji's attitude toward his daughter is entirely different. No sooner is she born than he starts scheming to marry her to the crown prince. Genji is not personally ambitious. It's just that no one else could possibly be good enough. The daughter doesn't have to work for anything or earn anything. All she has to do is be. Thanks to her father, she does become empress, but she remains a lifelong spoiled child, ruinously indulgent toward her favorite son, who looks just like Genji.

The Tale of Genji teems with spoiled daughters, many left to fend for themselves when their fathers die or fall from power. One daughter of a prince inherits a fine estate but is too helpless to run it. She stays on like some character out of a William Faulkner novel, quietly despairing while the house decays around her and the servants drift away to better places.

When Daddy Is No Longer There

So it matters little what century or society the pampering father and his spoiled daughter inhabit. Every spoiled daughter's destiny is encapsulated in the joke about the healthy little girl in the wheelchair.

As a child, she has the capacity to walk, but "Thank God, she doesn't have to." Yet, how many get through life without eventually having to stand on their own two feet? When that time comes for the girl in the wheelchair, she may well find that her legs have lost the power to support her.

No loving father who recognized his daughter's full humanity would cripple her in this manner. The problem lies in the fact that the pampering father does not recognize his daughter's full humanity or realize the harm that he is doing.

5

THE PYGMALION FATHER AND HIS COMPANION DAUGHTER

◆

"My Antigone!"

—Freud to his daughter, Anna

The Bookmaker's Daughter

Once upon a time, when Shirley Abbott was a little girl, a magical thing happened. She was doing some mending for her mother, when her father came into the room. He took the needle from her hands and replaced it with the key to his library. From now on, he meant, no more woman's work for her. From now on, she would develop her mind.

In her compelling autobiography, *The Bookmaker's Daughter*, Shirley Abbott examines how that day of fairy-tale transformation changed her life. An only child growing up in the border South, she had adored her lonely, bitter dreamer of a father. Now she became his chosen companion.[1]

For almost a decade, Shirley and her father shared one life. They dreamed together about Athens and Carthage and Rome, and talked about the grown-up books he gave her. Shirley's father was Yankee by birth and a bookie by profession, whereas

95

her mother was an uneducated "hillbilly." The Great Depression was on, and the family just managed to scrape by. To the town, they were barely a step above "white trash." But what did Shirley care? She and her father lived in a far better world than Arkansas.

Their happiness lasted until Shirley was in her late teens—in fact, until the day her acceptance to college arrived. Shirley was enthralled. Maybe all those dreams could be turned into reality.

To her shock, however, her father did not rejoice with her. As long as college had been a distant dream, he had encouraged her to plan for it. Now that it had become real, he couldn't bear to let her go.

Here was a turning point for Shirley Abbott as momentous as the day she traded in the needle for the key. She adored her father and felt she owed him everything. How could she hurt him by going away? How could she hope to be happy at his expense? Yet how could she sacrifice her whole future to his demands and not resent him for it?

In the end, Shirley Abbott went to college, then on to a successful career as a writer and publisher. But she and her father were never close in the same way again.

True and Toxic Mentoring

It should have been such a gratifying relationship. Here was a father who fostered his daughter's abilities and a daughter who repaid his efforts with gratitude and achievement. How could they have ended up like that?

In fact, the partnership of pygmalion father and companion daughter always ends up like that, with one or the other being sacrificed. The only unusual element in the Abbott case was that the sacrificed party wasn't the daughter. With great difficulty, Shirley Abbott separated her personhood from her daughterhood and affirmed her right to a future. A generation or two earlier, such a choice would have seemed unthinkable.

Toxic Mentors

The pygmalion father is a mentor, and mentors come in two varieties. One is the *true mentor*, who trains his disciples for independence; the other is the *toxic mentor* who trains them for lifelong discipleship.

A toxic-mentor father educates his daughter to serve his needs, not hers. He uses his prestige as man and parent to prey on her sense of insignificance. He teaches her that 1) as a female, she can't expect much from life, but that 2) as his daughter, a partial exception can be made. If these lessons take, she buys into the notion of herself as a lost soul, reclaimed through her father's godlike grace.

Toxic mentoring may include much genuine love. Pygmalion fathers truly believe that they are offering their daughters a very rare opportunity, and that by serving his needs she will also serve her own. Yet when a choice must be made between his needs and hers, the toxic mentor assumes that his come first.

Like Shirley Abbott's father, most toxic mentors are gifted, opinionated, emotionally isolated, and generally contemptuous of women, their wives most of all. They tend to be *imposing* men, in both senses of the term. Visionaries and teachers, they spellbind their impressionable daughters, who are bound to them by gratitude and admiration. Toxic mentors prefer disciples to colleagues. They want companions clever enough to admire their ideas but not confident enough to challenge them. Who could be more ideal than a bright, adoring daughter?

Sigmund and Anna

Because toxic mentors tend to be intellectuals, it's only to be expected that some very impressive figures have had companion daughters.

Sigmund Freud was a toxic mentor. Believing women to be incapable of mental growth past the age of thirty, he thought them unfit for careers. The emotionally healthy woman, he often said, is content with a home and family. His own daughter, Anna, of course was an exception. [2,3]

The youngest and cleverest of Freud's six children, Anna grew into womanhood during the early years of the twentieth century. Her father himself trained her as a psychoanalyst. Over the years, one male disciple after another broke with Freud over theoretical or leadership issues, but Anna remained orthodox and loyal. She also served as his nurse during his twenty-year struggle with oral cancer. After his death in 1939, she continued to promote his ideas.

Freud praised Anna as "my Antigone," recalling the selfless caretaker daughter of Oedipus. Although she fell in love several times, Anna never married and apparently never had sex. Freud fretted that Anna was going to be lonely after he was gone, but his actions spoke louder than his words. During his long illness, he permitted no one else to tend him, even when it came to the most sickening, arduous tasks. If he was going through a bad time, Anna canceled clients and even withdrew from conventions where she was scheduled to speak. It was understood that she was his companion first, a professional woman second, and a person with a private life last of all—if at all.

Over the years, Anna almost entirely usurped her mother's position. She became Freud's primary hostess and traveling companion. Freud did not exactly quarrel with his wife but withdrew from her lack of interest in his ideas. His mother had adored him and thought everything he did was wonderful. So Freud trained Anna to behave like his mother.

Anna was clever enough to understand his ideas, adoring enough to support him in everything he wanted, and emotionally dependent enough to commit her life to him. She was, in short, the ideal companion daughter.

Leo and Sasha

Leo Tolstoy, the world-famed Russian novelist, was Freud's older contemporary.[4] His opinion of women was considerably more hostile than Freud's. In the last decades of his life, he habitually pictured women as evil animals out to tempt men into sin and mindless breeding. He furiously condemned feminism and any suggestion of sexual equality. Women were incapable of a moral life, he said; they should be legally barred from all professions except prostitution.

The older Tolstoy grew, the more fanatic he became and the more vehemently he identified sex with sin. He loathed his wife, Sonia, in part because she dared to argue with him, but even more because she kept producing babies. He felt embarrassed before the world, proclaiming the virtues of chastity yet still fathering a baby every year.

In his old age, Leo Tolstoy published women-baiting parables like *The Kreutzer Sonata,* threw tantrums when his children married, and wrote his daughter Tanya that he'd rather see them all catch diphtheria, typhus, or scarlet fever than fall in love.[5]

Oddly enough, Tolstoy's favorite child was his youngest daughter, Sasha, whose birth had embarrassed him so badly. Sasha adored him right back and supported him in his endless quarrels with her mother. She even favored his plan to disown his whole family, herself included, as a protest against the institutions of private property and marriage. She even agreed with his decision, at ninety-plus, to leave home and become a wandering beggar. This decision killed him, but she still thought it was noble and right.

Loyal to the death, Sasha went through the rest of her life without ever marrying or making peace with her mother.

The Irony of the Companion Daughter's Role

Anna Freud and Sasha Tolstoy demonstrate the supreme irony of the companion daughter's role. Compared to neglected, abused, or even spoiled daughters, they seem fortunate. They are not only praised and favored, they are also well educated and taken seriously. Many have careers, sometimes important ones, and few get tied down with families. Yet, in the final analysis, they are little more than highly privileged slaves, house servants rather than field hands.

Danielle and Dad

If Sasha Tolstoy or Anna Freud had an inkling of their slave status, they never revealed it but went on devotedly serving. Today's companion daughters, however, often become uneasy enough to seek therapy. They tend to begin by expressing great puzzlement over their unhappiness. How could they be so miserable when they have such wonderful fathers? Yet it seldom takes long for the buried fury to surface.

Tall, blue-eyed Danielle was thirty when she decided to seek help. All her life, she and her father, Dan, had shared an intense closeness that excluded her mother. From the time she was eight, the two of them had traveled and attended the theater and opera together. After graduating from college, she had gone straight into his industrial real estate leasing agency. He had trained her, supervised her deals, invested her earnings, and turned her into an independently wealthy woman.

"What do you want to change?" I asked her.

She burst into tears. "I want to get out of industrial real estate. I hate it. I've always hated it. I want to open an art gallery. I want to take a vacation with someone else besides my father. I want to get married and have a family before it's too late. I want a life of my own."

"Who's stopping you?" I asked.

She became immediately defensive.

"It's not my dad, if that's what you mean. He's made me secure enough so I don't even have to work if I don't want to. He bought me my own condo. He encourages me to go out. He even advises me on how to keep men interested."

"What does he advise?"

She turned red. "He told me, 'Suck their cocks if you want to keep them.' "

In a way, Danielle was right. It wasn't her father who was keeping her from having the life she wanted. It was the dynamic between them, including her own attitude. She had allowed her father's choices to dominate every aspect of her existence, from the size of her bank account to where she lived to her activities in bed. She had money, privilege, and opportunity but no confidence whatever that she could function on her own. In her heart, Danielle feared that if she tried running an art gallery, she would surely fail, and if she gave up sexual catering, she would never hold any man's interest. Considering how little self she had, these fears were not unreasonable.

Danielle was motivated enough to make rapid progress in her therapy. Within a year, she had opened her gallery and was engaged to be married. When her father first became angry, then depressed, it was hard for her to cope. Even so, she continued to go her own way. Therapy helped her to understand that he was trying to force on her a set of rules that required one or the other of them to be sacrificed. But these were *his* rules and she was not obliged to accept them.

Accepting Womanhood

Companion daughters suffer terrible guilt if they try to assert themselves. Even more painful, sometimes, is the fear of losing their special status and becoming like lesser women.

So long as a companion daughter remains under her father's spell, she dares not sympathize with other women or identify herself as one of them. She learns to see them as negative models, images of what not to become. Shirley Abbott's father had taught her to be ashamed of her mother's lack of education and hillbilly ways. Not until her career was launched and she was a mother herself did Shirley realize that many of her own best qualities—her integrity, realism, and commitment to family—had been learned from her mother.

Wotan and Brünnhilde

One of the most powerful of all Mentoring Father–Companion Daughter stories is Richard Wagner's opera *Die Walküre*, first performed in 1870. Based on an ancient Germanic myth, *Die Walküre* tells of the king of the gods, Wotan, and his semi-divine daughter, Brünnhilde, who can only keep her goddess-like status as long as she repudiates all things feminine.

Brünnhilde is Wotan's favorite child, a warrior and an eternal virgin. She serves her father with joy, and he lavishes approval upon her. But their companionship ends the first time that she disobeys him. Regretfully but implacably, Wotan strips Brünnhilde of her immortality, puts her in a trance, surrounds her with a ring of fire, and offers her up as a sexual prize to the first hero who can reach her. After many twists and turns of plot, the story concludes with Brünnhilde's suicide.

And what had she done to deserve being reduced from amazon goddess to a helpless piece of meat? She had spared the life of her pregnant half-sister, Sieglinde. Sieglinde had committed adultery with her own twin brother, a crime of passion if ever there was one. Brünnhilde's own crime was to sympathize with her passionate sister instead of despising her. The punishment that Wotan chose reduced her to the status of an ordinary mortal female: passive, confined, a sex object, doomed to await rescue by a man, to fall in love, to suffer the agonies of desire and jealousy, and finally to die for her man.

Lermontov and Vicky

In *Die Walküre,* the daughter's powers are not really her own. They are gifts of the father, who has bestowed them and can take them away at will. They have strings attached; they can only be kept at the price of total submission.

The classic ballet film, *The Red Shoes,* made in 1947, plays out the same themes among human beings instead of gods. Vicky, a dedicated but unsuccessful dancer, is discovered by Lermontov, the world's greatest impresario. Vicky is an orphan, living with a silly aunt whom the misogynist Lermontov despises on sight. Lermontov rescues her from the aunt and becomes her surrogate father. Overnight, he turns an insecure unknown into a renowned dancer, in exchange for her promise to live only for the dance.

But Vicky does not keep her promise. When she falls in love with the company's resident composer, Lermontov banishes them both.

Vicky tries dancing for other companies, but her magic is gone. Desperate, she returns to Lermontov, who promises to make her the greatest dancer who ever lived—but only if she will leave her husband. Unable to choose, she kills herself.

The Red Shoes is based on a fairy tale and feels like a fairy tale. Lermontov is a magician who can turn Vicky into a princess, or back into a scullery maid again. Like Wotan, he can grant superhuman powers to a woman, but only at the price of her personhood. "I will do the talking," Lermontov tells Vicky. "You will do the dancing."

A classic companion daughter, Vicky believes that the mentor-father is the source of her achievement, even her identity. In contrast, her husband, the composer, is delighted to get away from Lermontov and writes greater and greater music as a result. The night of Vicky's suicide is the same night that his opera makes its triumphant debut.

The Seventh Veil, a film made around the same time as *The Red Shoes*, tells a similar story. This time, the mentor is a great piano teacher and the student is a female pianist. When she takes a stab at independence, he beats her hands with his cane, a reminder that her talent is his to foster or destroy. She flees his cruelty but comes back to him in the end.

In *The Seventh Veil* and *The Red Shoes*, the gifted girls are presented sympathetically. They are victimized by their mentors and have every reason to want to flee. Yet there is never any doubt that without their mentors the girls will revert to mediocrity. A talented man, like Vicky's composer husband, will outgrow his need for a mentor, but a woman won't. In the end, she will be forced to choose between womanhood and accomplishment, and whichever choice she makes will harm her.

Gappers

Die Walküre is derived from an ancient legend and *The Red Shoes* from a fairy tale. Surely their discouraging messages are not meant to apply to modern women!

And yet they do. All women today start with two disadvantages. The so-called "glass ceiling" keeps them out of positions of power, while salary structures reward them with about a third less pay than men receive for comparable work. Having a family adds yet another disadvantage.

In a 1992 study of almost 2,426 full-time career women age thirty to sixty-five, economists Joyce Jacobsen of Rhodes College and Laurence Levin of Santa Clara University concluded that women are never allowed to make up for interruptions in their careers.[6] Even twenty years after a return from a single six-month absence, "gappers" were making 10 percent less money than peers who had never left at all.

Because 85 percent of the "gaps" had been due to "family reasons," the implication is clear: Wotan and Lermontov are still in charge of the workplace.

Pygmalion and Galatea, Henry and Eliza

Stories like *Die Walküre* and *The Red Shoes* continue to stir and disturb us because their message still rings true: that even the most gifted women are men's creations and will be destroyed if they defy them.

This belief is very ancient. Athena, patron goddess of Athens, sprang directly from the head of Zeus. Motherless and eternally a virgin, she became a living extension of her father's will. She ruled over Athens, but only as his viceroy, his representative. By herself, she was nothing.

Zeus was not the only legendary male capable of creating just the female he wanted. The sculptor Pygmalion made a statue of an ideal beauty, fell in love with her, then brought her to life. In myths like these, the daughter is literally the father's brainchild, born from his mind instead of from a woman's body.

In many such stories, the father-creator-mentor eventually becomes the lover, just as Pygmalion did. In Lady Murasaki's *Tale of Genji*, a young man of twenty adopts a beautiful orphan girl of ten, educates her exactly to his taste, then marries her. Here is the reality of which Pygmalion legends are made.

Mentoring men deeply enjoy educating a woman and taking credit for her achievements—so long as she doesn't start seeing herself as their equal or imagining she can get along without them. George Bernard Shaw's comedy *Pygmalion,* a satirical updating of the original legend, mocks this tendency.

To win a bet, the self-centered, middle-aged linguist, Henry Higgins, gives elocution lessons to the Cockney flower girl, Eliza, and passes her off as a lady. Weary of his arrogance, Eliza runs off with a naive but adoring suitor, planning to open her own elocution school. The play ends with the furious Higgins assuring himself that she is bound to fail and come crawling back.

The Lermontov-and-Vicky dance all over again? Not this time.

Shaw, who loved to turn accepted notions on their heads, wrote a commentary on *Pygmalion.* The resourceful Eliza, he said, was right to leave the overbearing Higgins. Rather than failing without his help, she would succeed and be happy. Spunky women like Eliza don't need dominating men, said Shaw. They are much better off with men they can dominate, as Eliza dominates Freddie.

But patriarchal stereotypes die hard. When *Pygmalion* was turned into a musical, *My Fair Lady,* the ending was rewritten so that Eliza left Freddie and went back to Higgins after all. Audiences worldwide thought it was wonderfully romantic. Even today, successful women tend to look for men who are even more successful than they are, in order to cast them in the mentor role.

Yet Shaw was right. Necessary and useful as they may be to their apprentices, *mentors are meant to be outgrown.* A teacher who can't let his student graduate, a mentor who won't let his apprentice become independent, is toxic.

Taking a Good Thing Too Far

Nothing is more beautiful than a Mentoring Father-Companion Daughter relationship—within limits. Fathers can be inspiring teachers, and daughters love to learn from them. The problem arises when it's time for the daughter to graduate and either the father or the daughter (or both) refuses to let go.

A century or two ago, this problem would never have been recognized as a problem. Women were expected to spend their lives in service to a man. Whether she served her father or a husband made no difference. In those days, a young girl like Shirley Abbott would have been seen as monstrously selfish for putting her own wishes first.

The heyday of the companion daughter was from the mid-nineteenth century through the early twentieth, a period that coincided with the first phases of female emancipation. Previous to that time, women were deemed too unintelligent to be worthy companions for brilliant men. A father like John Milton might use his daughters as secretaries and nurses, but he would never have expected them to understand his ideas. The post-Enlightenment improvement in women's status and education changed all that. Although women were still socially subservient, the realization had dawned that some of them had intelligence. Women might not be capable of originating ideas, it was thought, but at least they could understand and admire them.

Companion-daughter types began showing up in numbers in Victorian fiction, serious but modest girls like Agnes in Dickens's *David Copperfield,* the mainstay first of her father, later of her husband. In *Middlemarch,* George Eliot's Dorothea Brooke weds a cranky scholar three times her age so that she can help him in his research. An idealistic orphan repelled by the trite servitude of an ordinary marriage, yet denied the opportunity to do serious work of her own, she marries a toxic-mentor father surrogate. Dorothea's choice helps to explain why so many companion daughters never leave their fathers, and also why fatherless young women, such as Oona O'Neill, Carol Marcus, and Gloria Vanderbilt, are sometimes so powerfully attracted to accomplished older men.

If companion daughters are fading from the scene today, it's because of the better options and improved opportunities now

106

open to women. It's a measure of just how much things have changed that it's now Shirley Abbott's father and not Shirley who strikes us as selfish.

Scott, Zelda, Scottie, and Sheilah

Just as some young women look for father-surrogates to mentor them, some men look for daughter substitutes to mentor. The brilliant, alcoholic, Jazz Age novelist F. Scott Fitzgerald, author of *The Great Gatsby* and *Tender Is the Night,* had a powerful urge to mentor women, but only women he could dominate.

His first significant student was his future wife, Zelda, a glamorous Southern belle who was only seventeen when they met during the First World War. Zelda, however, always wanted to apply what she was taught, to start writing as she learned more about literature, to start painting as she learned more about art.

In her biography, *Zelda,* Nancy Milford describes the tragic outcome. Scott was threatened by her ambitions and even took stories that she wrote and published them under his own name. The marriage turned nightmarish, and Zelda had a breakdown from which she never fully recovered.

Scott next started mentoring his daughter, Scottie, giving her lists of books to read and telling her in advance how to interpret them. He also told her what habits, manners, and people to cultivate and which to avoid. Scottie was an affectionate child, but no girl in her teens wants to be endlessly lectured, and she let her impatience show.

Then Scott Fitzgerald found the perfect female disciple. While his wife languished in a mental hospital and his daughter was at boarding school, he began an affair with Sheilah Graham, formerly an orphan child of the Cockney slums, now an aspiring Hollywood gossip columnist. The beautiful and bright Sheilah had already been mentored by earlier lovers. She now yearned for the polish of an education, and Scott was only too glad to help.

A Princeton graduate, and the famed chronicler of upper-class

107

life, Scott was an awesome figure to Sheilah. He became her tutor-father-lover and she his student-daughter-mistress, and both loved their roles. When Scott got drunk, he could be cruelly offensive, but when he sobered up, he was the finest, most patient teacher imaginable. He died in his mid-forties, while they were still lovers and before she outgrew her need for him as a mentor. She later had quite a happy life, which included a lucrative career and a family. But she always saw her time with Scott Fitzgerald as the crowning point of her existence, and years later wrote a loving and grateful memoir, *Beloved Infidel.*

Tom and Sally

So, not all men who mentor women are toxic to them. In *Passionate Attachments*, her collection of in-depth studies of father-daughter pairs, Signe Hammer presents us with the very attractive example of Dr. Tom Archway, a physician, and his daughter, Sally, who became one of America's first female Episcopal priests.[7]

Serious-minded Sally was the elder of Tom's two daughters. From the time she was small, he gave her a great deal of attention. He took her rafting, brought her to his clinic on Saturday mornings, and told her that the most important thing for a woman, as for a man, was to be able to support herself. It was no secret that he hoped Sally would become a doctor and join his practice.

When she chose the seminary instead, he was stunned. A lifelong agnostic, he couldn't imagine his daughter as a priest. His first reaction was to tell her she was "screwing up her life."[8] Fortunately, it did not take him long to remember his liberal principles. Calming down, he added, "Roosevelt said we all have four freedoms. Roosevelt was wrong, we have five. And the fifth freedom is to screw up our lives."[9] In other words, he conceded that Sally's future was her own to decide.

Tom Archway had almost made Sally's decision into a cause for estrangement, but he backed off in time. From that point on, he supported her in her choice, much as if she were preparing for a career that he would have liked better. By the time she was ordained, he was able to rejoice with her and to recognize that she was happy. He didn't become religious himself, or really understand what was driving her, and she never insisted that he must. Instead, they allowed each other to be separate people with differing feelings and values, who did not have to account to each other.

Happy Endings

Of all the stories recounted in this chapter, Tom and Sally's is the only one with a truly happy ending because it's the only one in which neither the father nor the daughter had to be sacrificed. It's a hopeful story because it's also a late-twentieth-century story. It tells us that some fathers and daughters are actually learning to dance new steps together and that the steps, fortunately, can be learned.

6

THE RUINED FATHER AND HIS RESCUING DAUGHTER

◆

CORDELIA: O dear father,
It is thy business that I go about . . .

GENTLEMAN (*to Lear*): Thou hast one daughter
Who redeems nature from the general
curse . . .

—Shakespeare, *King Lear*

A Scavenger for Love

Shari's agitation was obvious the moment she came through the door. A thin, high-strung young woman of twenty-eight, she still had her neck in a brace, the result of a car crash two months before. She was at a turning point in her career, she said, her pale eyes swimming with tears. She had a job with a music publisher. A short time ago, she had been promoted and given a challenging new assignment, but she had already missed a deadline and forgotten an important meeting. Her boss had forgiven her because of her accident, but he was a businessman, not a saint. If she didn't straighten out soon, she was going to blow her career.

"It didn't really start with the accident," she confessed. "I was already on a downward spiral. The reason I wasn't watching the road was because I was thinking about my boyfriend, who has

111

AIDS. Actually, things had been going sour with us even before he was diagnosed. He'd been shooting drugs, which is how he got AIDS in the first place. Anyway, we'd been drifting so far apart that I was thinking of leaving him, but when I found out he was sick, I blamed everything on that. To be perfectly honest, though, the relationship's been in trouble since the beginning."

"You've been tested for AIDS?" I asked.

She nodded. "Oh, of course. I'm negative, at least so far. I'm not really worried. I never worry about myself. But now I have to, don't I? I mean, what's to become of us if I can't work? But how can I keep my mind on my work with all this going on? David's so angry and withdrawn all the time. I can't get through to him. I try to comfort him but it's useless. I don't know how much more I can take."

"How was it with your father when you were a child?" I asked her.

She sighed. "Oh, we got along fine, though I wouldn't say we were ever that close. Dad was a research scientist. His work took up all his time. I tried to please him by being the perfect daughter, excelling in everything, never missing a day at school. Everything was cool until I was in the sixth grade and his project lost its funding. He'd been on it twelve years and had gotten so specialized that he couldn't get anything else. Anyway, he never found another job. We had to live on what my mom could make, while he sank into this pitiful depression and quit even looking for work.

"I tried to help out by asking for as little as possible. We had our ten-year high-school class reunion a few months ago. A group of us were discussing what we remembered about one another. Someone said he would never forget how wan and shabby I always looked, like a kid in an ad for adopting a Third World child.

"I worried about Dad all the time. I'd try to get close, but he'd say, *Don't bother me now.* Then I got bronchitis and had to stay home. I loved being alone with him, even if he hardly noticed I was there. He was on antidepressants and totally out of it, really, but I felt my mere presence was good for him. After that, I'd make up excuses to cut school so I could be near him."

Shari's experience with her father had trained her in martyrdom to an ill, depressed, and unavailable man. As a child, she tried to win his attention with rescuing behavior. Now she was doing the same with her lover. Sacrificing herself to rescue a man was what her life was all about.

Antigone and Oedipus

Women like Shari are the inheritors of a long tradition. As far back as we go, we find women very like her. Twenty-five hundred years ago, the Athenian playwright Sophocles immortalized one of her most famous forebears: Antigone, the daughter of King Oedipus, heroine of the play named for her.

Oedipus, abandoned as an infant, unknowingly kills his father and marries his mother when he grows up, thereby becoming king. When the truth is revealed, he blinds himself and flees into exile. Defying an edict, Antigone seeks him out to be his nurse and guide. She is arrested but bravely escapes and joins him again. After Oedipus's death, she goes home only to discover that one of her brothers has been killed in a failed revolt. Her uncle Creon, now king, refuses to let the brother be buried. Unable to persuade Creon to change his mind, Antigone performs the funeral herself and is condemned and executed.

Antigone is a powerhouse of a heroine. For thousands of years, her name has been synonymous with unshakable integrity and the willingness to defy unjust laws and die for a principle. Athens was a profoundly antifeminist society. Why should Sophocles have embodied such magnificent traits in a woman?

The answer lies in the principle Antigone dies for. Her one and only purpose in breaking the law is to serve her father and her brothers. Antigone cares nothing for politics or dynastic struggles. She cares nothing for women either, least of all herself. She simply carries out her programming as relentlessly as a cyborg in a *Terminator* movie. Marilyn French, author of *The Women's Room,* has observed that while Antigone is the central character, Creon is the human one. He is faulty, changeable, and faced with moral

113

choices, while she is so perfect, fearless, and incorruptible that we can never imagine her swerving from her intent.

Antigone is not a person but an embodiment of the ideal Greek daughter. For her, there are no choices, no moral dilemmas. Her duty is plain: to serve her father and brothers, whatever the cost to herself. Creon, the man, must deal with ethical conflicts, but Antigone's only choice is whether to do her duty or not. For a woman of integrity, that's really not a choice at all. She does her duty, even if it means dying for it.

In short, the ideal Greek daughter was a voluntary human sacrifice.

Cordelia and Lear

Two thousand years later, the ideal daughter was still sacrificing herself. In Shakespeare's *King Lear,* she is embodied in Cordelia.

Lear opens with a scene at court. The aging king plans to hand over his property to his daughters, announce Cordelia's engagement, and then retire. First, however, he demands a little ritual. His daughters must tell the world how much they love him. Although married, the two older daughters swear that their hearts belong exclusively to Daddy. Honest Cordelia, his favorite, refuses to play the game. After assuring her father of her appreciation for all he has done for her, she adds:

> Why have my sisters husbands, if they say
> They love you all? Haply, when I shall wed,
> That Lord whose hand must take my plight shall carry
> Half my love with him, half my care and duty . . .

Lear explodes. He disowns Cordelia and exiles her from Britain. When the king of France marries her without a dowry, he is furious.

Lear carries on like a toddler asked to share his mother's affec-

114

tion with a new brother. Luckily for him, Cordelia is a selflessly devoted, unconditionally loving daughter-mother. When Lear is later beggared and cast out by her sisters, Cordelia leads an army to his rescue, planning to nurse him back to health. When she finds him, he makes the nearest approach to an apology of which he is capable:

LEAR:
If you have poison for me, I will drink it.
I know you do not love me; for your sisters
Have, as I do remember, done me wrong:
You have some cause, they have not.

CORDELIA:
No cause, no cause.

This exchange is the key to the play. Lear's elder daughters threw him out to die; that, of course, is monstrous and unforgivable. Lear previously threw Cordelia out to die; that, of course, is "no cause" for a daughter to hold a grudge. Instead, she risks her life to save him, like a mother whose baby is in danger.

In the first scene, Cordelia had argued for her right to love her husband. In the final scenes, she forgets all about him. The emotional goal of the play is to restore Cordelia to Lear so that they can die together like lovers—like *Romeo and Juliet*—the girl in the man's arms.

So, Lear's favorite daughter is not merely his child, she is also his mother and his lover. She exists to serve his needs and to sacrifice her life for him. Their relationship is anything but equal. Her loyalty, love, and forgiveness are unconditional; his depend on whether she pleases him or not. Yet Lear is the one we feel for, the one who seems human and comprehensible. How can we possibly identify with someone as superhumanly noble as Cordelia? As Marilyn French said of Antigone, she's too "absolute, static, inflexible."[1]

115

Dombey and Daughter

If we now fast-forward two hundred and fifty more years to the Victorian period, we find the rescuing daughter still on the job. The difference is that she has now been partially humanized and granted feelings. If she expresses no anger over the horrible abuse that she suffers, at least she does feel pain, grief, confusion, and fear.

In the ironically named *Dombey and Son*, Dickens's Mr. Dombey needs a male offspring to inherit the family business. His daughter, Florence, means so little to him that he puts "only child of" on the tombstone of her brother, Paul. Abandoned by her father, motherless Florence survives through the kindness of servants and strangers, finally marrying a nice, if humble, fellow. Then Dombey's business fails, his health collapses, and he is left a broken man. As soon as Florence hears this news, she rushes to his side. He begs her forgiveness, she grants it joyfully, and they live happily ever after.

Credible? Not very. Yet, at the age of twelve, father-abandoned Germaine Greer "cried [herself] blind" when she read *Dombey and Son*.[2] Great writers such as Dickens and Shakespeare move us because they tap into our most powerful irrational yearnings, yearnings fed by a family culture that makes conflict inevitable and resolution hard. Lear's reconciliation with Cordelia and Dombey's with Florence are what we want for ourselves but fear we will never achieve. And so we weep.

We have now almost reached the present day, Shari's day. But there is one transitional example to look at before we get there.

The Belle of Atlanta

Margaret Mitchell, author of *Gone With the Wind*, had a remarkable mother.[3] May Belle Stephens Mitchell was an active suffragist and a founder of what was to become the League of Women Voters. She was also a founder and leader of the Atlanta Women's

Study Club and an organizer (and the first female member) of the Catholic Layman's Association, formed to oppose the racist demagogue Tom Watson. May Belle herself had been the child of a powerful mother, Annie Fitzgerald Stephens, an entrepreneur who rebuilt her family's fortunes after the Civil War and became her grandchild's model for Scarlett O'Hara.

As a parent, May Belle Mitchell was stern, demanding, and somewhat insensitive. Margaret was only six when May Belle started warning her about the perils for women of relying on men instead of themselves. May Belle dismissed Margaret's desire to write as too feminine and impractical; she wanted her daughter to go North for her education and become a professional, preferably a doctor. Margaret admired her mother, but not always her mother's opinions.

May Belle died in the great flu epidemic of 1918, when Margaret was an eighteen-year-old freshman at Smith. At the time, Margaret was still grieving over the death of her fiancé, a cultivated and patrician New Yorker, killed in France during World War I. Overwhelmed, she quit college and went home to Atlanta, returning to her father's household.

On her deathbed, May Belle had roused herself to write Margaret a warning: "Your father loves you dearly, but [he] has lived his life . . . ; never let his or anyone else's life interfere with your real life."[4] Her concern was well-founded. Yet Margaret ignored her mother's wishes, first by quitting college and later by submitting to her father's domination.

Eugene Mitchell was as impressive as his wife. A highly civic-minded attorney, he held positions with the Atlanta Historical Society, the Atlanta and the Georgia Bar Associations, the Democratic party, and other organizations. By temperament, he was aloof, reserved, and formal. Margaret was immensely proud to be his daughter but always had trouble attracting his attention.

If she had hoped to get closer to him now that her mother was dead, she was disappointed. Perhaps as a reaction, she set out on a career of Jazz Age hell-raising that would have done credit to

117

Zelda Fitzgerald. Pretty and vivacious, she attended wild parties, drank heavily, married a bootlegger, broke into the all-male stronghold of newspaper reporting, interviewed celebrities like Valentino, divorced her bootlegger after he beat her so badly that she landed in the hospital, then settled down with a conventional and hardworking second husband who adored her.

Soon after her second marriage, Margaret quit journalism and spent the next ten years writing *Gone With the Wind*, apparently with no intention to publish. What she wrote was personal and even autobiographical: the experience of being a teenaged girl during wartime; the quarrel with respectable society; events from her family's history; the experience of rushing home to a sick mother, only to find her dead; the character of Ashley, partially based on her slain fiancé; the character of Rhett, partially based on her bootlegger husband. As she wrote, she considered many of the issues that plagued her: rebellion versus conformity, self-assertion versus self-sacrifice, feminist revolt versus patriarchal values.

A college friend who worked at Macmillan pressed her into submitting the unfinished manuscript. A year later, at thirty-six, Margaret Mitchell woke up rich and famous. The experience not only astonished but appalled her. Instead of running to meet her success, she turned and fled it, and her major escape became nursing her father.

Eugene Mitchell's health broke down soon after *Gone With the Wind* was published, and Margaret spent the next eight years being his primary care giver. Despite her relative youth, Margaret was hardly in any shape to tend an invalid. Suffering from arthritis, eye problems, migraine headaches, allergies, a bad back, and a series of accidents, there were times she could hardly drag herself out of bed. Her husband also needed attention, having suffered a near-fatal heart attack. Yet, her father's demands always came first.

According to Margaret's biographer, Darden Asbury Pyron, Eugene Mitchell would not go into the hospital unless his daughter went with him. He imposed on her the "primary care-giving responsibilities . . . bathing him and feeding him,"[5] and moving him around physically. According to another source, when a ball was given by the Junior League to honor the Atlanta premiere of the film, Margaret excused herself to be with her father.[6] Her labors exacerbated her own health problems, especially damaging her back.

Plainly, Margaret Mitchell was playing the kind of Victorian "Angel in the House" that she had embodied in Ellen and Melanie. These saintly characters died young of their self-sacrifices, but while they lived they were rewarded with vast love and appreciation. No doubt, Margaret expected the same reward from her father. Eugene, however, gave her little but complaints and cantankerousness. Margaret's biographers portray this whole period as miserable and her state of mind as bitter. In the end, she outlived her father by a mere three years and never wrote again.

Switching Dances

The Mitchells' story demonstrates how easily father-daughter dancers may switch from one dance to another. For nearly forty years, Eugene and Margaret had been a typical Distant Father/ Yearning Daughter pair. Along the way, she had tried to lure him into a Mentoring Father/Companion Daughter dance, by running his household and by emulating his interest in literature and history; but he had failed to follow her lead.

Then, when his health collapsed, *he* changed the dance. A better man might have gone the way of Kagekiyo—acknowledging his fault, blessing his child, letting her go. Margaret, in turn, might have hired him a nurse, visited him frequently, and still taken time to write and enjoy. She might even have let him hire his own nurse, which he had ample means to do. Nor did they ask her healthy brother, who also lived in Atlanta, to take over part of the burden.

Instead, they elected to do the Ruined Father-Rescuing Daughter routine. By following neglect with exploitation, Eugene compounded the harm he had already done, while Margaret sacrificed all the brilliant possibilities awaiting her in order to serve his insatiable demands.

Not Yet Gone With the Wind

Although Margaret Mitchell had never been her father's Companion Daughter, she still ended up as his nurse. Like Anna Freud, she put a significant career aside to play caretaker to her father.

Sigmund Freud and Eugene Mitchell were contemporaries. Born five thousand miles apart, they still shared the most fundamental expectations and values. Both knew that their daughters were brilliant and ambitious, yet considered a daughter's career of far less importance than a father's convenience. Both asked sacrifices of their daughters that they never would have asked of their sons. Even when their daughters were world-famous, both still perceived them as primarily domestic servants—nurturers, nurses.

Anna Freud clearly shared her father's assumptions, so for her the sacrifice was relatively easy. Besides, she and her father had already been close long before he became ill. Margaret Mitchell's circumstances had been different. The child of brilliant parents who seldom had time for her, she had not been close to either of them. Margaret never could decide whether she wanted to be Scarlett—the angry and ambitious rebel who goes her own way, or Melanie—the traditional nurturer whom everyone loves. Her ambivalence enriched her novel but circumscribed her life. *Gone With the Wind,* at once so naive and so powerful, captures the confusion and frustration of gifted women in a society that grudgingly permits them to achieve but does not value their achievements. The story retains its power today because the dilemma it embodies is still not gone with the wind.

Wee Nannies

Rescuing daughters often start their rescuing in childhood, like Shari, who stayed home from school to look after her despondent father. The Scottish call such caretaking children "Wee Nannies"—little substitute mothers. Wee Nannies spend their childhoods nurturing those who by all rights should be nurturing them.

There is something touching and sweet about the sight of Wee Nannies at work. In novels and films, they are always good for a flood of tears. In books like Dostoyevski's *Crime and Punishment* or Dickens's *Little Dorrit,* or Betty Smith's *A Tree Grows in Brooklyn,* the exploited Wee Nannie sees her hapless father as a gifted and extraordinary being who needs protection from a harsh world.

Even when Dostoyevski's Sonya becomes a prostitute, or when Little Dorrit has to go out to beg, or when Betty Smith's Francie doesn't eat for days, these Wee Nannies never blame their fathers. Shari was the same. Her poor father, she claimed, couldn't get another job after he was fired because he was such a brilliant specialist. She wouldn't allow herself to realize that a more adaptable man would have gone in for retraining.

As adults, Wee Nannies continue the habit of making excuses for male losers and sacrificing themselves. Sonia marries a convicted murderer and Little Dorrit chooses a man in debtor's prison. Shari picked a drug addict for a lover.

When rescuing daughters begin their rescuing late in life, as Margaret Mitchell did, the reason is usually that the father didn't need rescuing when she was small. From early childhood on, Margaret Mitchell was desperate for her father's attention. But so long as he was healthy, busy, and successful, she had no way of getting it.

Pseudo-Nurturing

In theory, children who are nurtured learn to nurture and children who are loved learn to love. How do we account for the nurturing capacity of the neglected daughter? How can she give back what she has never received?

Infants enter the world equipped to attract the care that they need. In the first days of life, they initiate bonds by gazing deeply into the eyes of the person holding them. Within two or three months, they vocalize and smile to court attention. Their smiles are invitations, meant to start an interaction and keep it going. As anthropologist Desmond Morris has observed, babies *get* attention by crying and *keep* it by smiling.[7]

Appearance adds to the appeal. Infants and children have rounder foreheads and cheeks, bigger eyes, and smaller noses and chins than adults. This configuration is known as the "Babyface" or *Kinderschema,* and acts as a signal for adults to smile and coo at, cuddle, and care for the little creature. Young puppies and kittens also have big eyes and small chins, which is one reason why people choose them for pets. Makers of dolls and puppets copy the babyface features, often exaggerating them.

But what happens when adults don't respond to these signals? If the emotional deprivation is severe enough, even the best-fed infant may die. Milder deprivation produces desperate attempts to attract attention, ranging from screaming fits to whining to becoming too good to be true.

The Wee Nannie's strategy is to court love and protection by modeling love and protection. If the father is the parent who is failing her, she tries to win him over by giving him care. Many rejected children also project their own needs onto some surrogate object, lavishing immense affection on a doll or a pet. In *Dombey and Son,* neglected Florence is fanatically devoted both to her rejecting father and her motherless baby brother.

Yet no child has the maturity to take care of a needy adult, especially if that adult is a ruined father. *Pseudo-nurturing* is the most she can give. On some level, she knows she'll never change her father, and she's right; he doesn't change.

Wee-Nannie Boys

There are male Wee Nannies, too, boys enslaved to the needs of a dependent parent, usually the mother. The difference is that the reader or audience almost always favors the son in his desire to break free from his enslavement. In D. H. Lawrence's *Sons and Lovers,* in Dominie Taylor's *Mother Love,* in Tennessee Williams's *The Glass Menagerie,* and in the hilarious film *Throw Mama from the Train,* the hero is waging a battle for his freedom, and the reader or audience only wishes he would fight harder. We want him to face the hopelessness of his situation and to *get out.*

Until the last few generations, however, readers and audiences were seldom asked to side with a daughter against a father. Even if the daughter had wanted to leave, where could she have gone? Prior to the late nineteenth century, a runaway boy could join the army, go to sea, start a business, learn a profession, or master a craft, but a runaway girl had no profession open to her but prostitution. In Richardson's *Clarissa,* once the persecuted heroine fled her home, her choice was limited to dishonor or death. Even servants had to be "respectable," and women who left their families lost their respectability. An adventurous man was admired, but the word *adventuress* was merely a polite term for whore.

So, the exploited daughter was stuck, unable either to change her situation or to leave it. From infancy on, life taught her helplessness and powerlessness and set her up for repetition compulsions. Yet this was the image of womanhood idealized by society.

Foul-Weather Annies

Some Wee Nannies grow up to be Foul-Weather Annies, women comfortable only when up to the neck in someone else's misery. Foul-Weather Annies are drawn to the needy, not the healthy. They seek out the helpless, not the happy. Full-time rescuers, they are lost without someone to "help."

Foul-Weather Annies form a substantial minority at meetings of Al-Anon or Co-Dependents Anonymous or Adult Children of Alcoholics and in helping professions such as teaching or nursing or social work—and on the pages of Melody Beattie's *Co-Dependent No More.* Unlike those who are moved by true compassion, Foul-Weather Annies are driven to help others out of their own desperate need for rescue. Society encourages them because they willingly do the jobs that few men want to do, and do them cheaply, because many people still believe that enabling others is woman's destiny.

Intermittent Reinforcement

There is a widespread tendency, by people as diverse as Freudians and feminists, to criticize women for rescuing behavior. The assumption is that women must be masochists or codependents to volunteer for such thankless tasks. Yet what often motivates them is actually hope, the hope of getting what Cordelia or Florence Dombey finally got.

Meanwhile, they live on the occasional smiles and thanks that serve to feed the hope. This phenomenon is called *intermittent reinforcement*,[8] and has been demonstrated with animals in laboratories. Once an animal has learned to press a certain lever to get food, it will continue to try getting food by pressing that lever, however rarely it actually comes. In fact, animals will work harder to get unpredictable rewards than those that come predictably. In much the same way, spouses or children will sometimes put more effort into pleasing someone who is hard to please than someone who is lavish with affection and appreciation.

So it's not necessarily masochism that keeps people in painful circumstances, but the value they place on the infrequent but valuable rewards that they do receive and the dream of getting what they're waiting for, somewhere down the line.

Most daughters learn early that their father's attention is both highly valuable and hard to win. This knowledge breeds a hunger to become worthy in the father's eyes. In the case of the rescuing daughter, the opportunity may not come until her father is down-and-out. His misery is her opportunity. That's the dark and rather frightening side of the rescuing-daughter's story.

7

THE ANGUISHED FATHER AND
HIS ANGRY DAUGHTER

◆

KING LEAR: When were you wont to be so
Full of songs, sirrah?
FOOL: . . . Ever since thou madest thy
Daughters thy mothers . . . when
Thou gavest them the rod and
Putt'st down thine own breeches . . .

—Shakespeare, *King Lear*

Lear and Goneril, Larry and Ginny

We have seen that Cordelia, King Lear's youngest child, is the ideal embodiment of the Rescuing Daughter. In contrast, her two older sisters, Goneril and Regan, are the most vengeful Angry Daughters imaginable. Before the play is over, they have ripped out the eyes of a sick old man, sent their father into the storm to die, assassinated their younger sister, and plotted to murder each other.

Yet, when we first meet them, Goneril and Regan seem like perfectly normal people. Like many of us, they accommodate their father when he's around and complain when he can't hear. In the opening scene, they watch in silence as Lear disowns, curses, and exiles Cordelia. Once alone, as most of us would, they put their heads together to assess the situation:

125

GONERIL:
He always loved our sister most; and with what
poor judgment he hath now cast her off appears too
grossly.

REGAN:
'Tis the infirmity of his age: yet he hath ever
but slenderly known himself.

What they say is the plain truth. In disowning Cordelia, Lear has certainly shown poor judgment and little self-knowledge and he may well be senile. He has already declared his intention to spend half of each month with each of his two elder daughters. He also plans to bring along a hundred friends and servants. Faced with such a prospect, what daughters wouldn't be feeling anxious?

The next time we see Goneril, she has just been told that Lear has struck one of her servants. She then attempts to draw some reasonable lines. First, she says, he is not to strike her servants, and second, he must end the nightly drunken parties which have transformed her home into "a tavern or a brothel." In response, Lear screams at her for dozens of lines, calling her a "degenerate bastard," a "marble-hearted fiend," and a vulture. He calls on Nature to make her barren, or else to curse her with children who will make her life a torment. "Blasts and fogs upon thee!" he shrieks. "A father's curse pierce every sense about thee!" All this because she asked him not to strike her servants or let his own get drunk every night.

Lear's behavior is so intolerable that, in order to sustain sympathy for him, Shakespeare must transform Goneril and Regan from the exasperated victims that they first appear to be into the unmitigated fiends their crazy father accuses them of being. But that is only one way of viewing the story.

In her Pulitzer Prize–winning 1991 novel, *A Thousand Acres*, Jane Smiley resets Shakespeare's story in Iowa, renaming Goneril Ginny and telling the events from her point of view. Larry, the Lear figure, is a family tyrant who disowns his favorite youngest daughter, then divides his property between Ginny and the middle sister, both farmers' wives. Smiley explores the hell of growing up the daughters of such an irascible father, empathizing with Ginny's plight, and showing how her father's behavior becomes so intolerable that she has little choice but to throw him out.

This is, of course, a frankly revisionist interpretation, one that asserts the equal claims of male and female, parent and child. Until quite recently, such a view of *King Lear* would have been unthinkable. *Of course* Lear had the right to bully, castigate, or disown his daughters. *Of course* his daughters were obliged to be patiently forgiving. *Of course* we should feel pity for him and outrage at his ill treatment, no matter what he did.

As a member of a society that took patriarchal values for granted, Shakespeare expected his audience to feel that way. Lear gives his daughters "all"—his entire wealth, property, and power— in the expectation that they will gratefully and indulgently love him for it. Instead, they take his gifts and send him into the storm to die. Lear can't comprehend it and goes mad with sorrow, shame, rage, disillusionment, and hurt. Goneril and Regan are treating their father the way their father had treated Cordelia, and Lear finally has the grace to understand this. "I did her wrong," he realizes, huddling with other homeless wretches in the rain. He also realizes that, as king, he never considered the needs of the poor. It's because he is capable of learning these lessons that Lear finally earns the audience's respect along with its pity.

In Lear, we see the example of a father who won't recognize his failings as a parent until forced to by suffering. We also see how a child's anger can grow cancerously out of control, evolving into a lust for destruction that ultimately destroys the child herself.

A Short History of Anger

The anger we see in *King Lear* is truly terrifying. It is a power sufficient to destroy a family, a nation, a world. Yet, when we believe we have been ill treated, how else are we to feel but angry?

Today, we are probably more confused about anger than about any other emotion. This was not always the case. In most times and places, the right to anger has been clearly determined by class and gender. The God of the Old Testament was almost continuously in a state of anger, or "righteous indignation." His wrath, of course, was not a fault in *Him;* the fault lay with those who made him angry with their defiance. On the earthly plane, human males in positions of authority permitted themselves a godlike freedom to lose their tempers and punish, again blaming the provocation of others. Thus, kings, husbands, fathers, teachers, nobles, and slave drivers all enjoyed the free expression of their anger. Among women, children, slaves, and other lowly beings, however, anger was considered an evil and ugly emotion, to be suppressed at all costs.

The reason for the discrepancy was simple: the anger of the lowly was perceived as rebellion. This is the ethos that shapes *King Lear.* Anger is the privilege of dominant males, and women have no right to it.

This ancient attitude still dominates much of our thinking. In many circles, punching people out is not only permissible to men but actually gives them status. This is not the case with women. On the job, men who occasionally lose their tempers are seen as behaving normally, while women who do the same are thought of as out of control. And the very parents who are most punitive toward their children are least likely to tolerate their children's expressing anger in return.

Yet there is also a whole other set of attitudes toward anger. Especially over the last century or two, a countermovement has developed—a very British and upper-class contempt for anger as womanish and self-indulgent, and therefore unfit for men. In circles most affected by this attitude, anger is seen as "uncool," a failure of control, a weakness. Men influenced by this concept cultivate a calm voice and a stoic manner. Even when inwardly furious, they proclaim that they aren't a bit angry, that they never

get angry. Many politicians, afraid to look like ranting dema-
gogues, try to appear inhumanly rational. In the United States and
England, voters would be almost as unlikely to elect someone who
showed his temper as someone who shed tears.

And yet, even this is not the whole story. In recent decades,
especially among groups that consider themselves disadvantaged,
anger has been perceived as fueling their campaign against injustice. From feminists to black liberationists to gay activists, and on
both sides of the abortion issue, some factions celebrate the necessity for anger and deliberately encourage it in their followers. Like
tyrants of old, they indulge in "righteous indignation," only this
time those who claim the right to be indignant are those who
oppose rather than uphold the *status quo.*

In *My Enemy, My Love: Man-hating and Ambivalence in Women's
Lives,* Judith Levine explains women's anger toward men as the
inevitable result of both their subordinate status as women and
their profound disappointment with their idealized fathers, who
have failed them through absence, inaccessibility, or abuse. The
daughters of such fathers are at once perfectionistic and cynical,
says Levine, demanding the impossible from men and becoming
vindictive when they don't get it.

The Uses and Abuses of Anger

So what *is* anger? A male privilege? A female weakness? A piece
of uncivilized behavior unworthy of a gentleman? A prerogative of
the mighty? A tool in the hands of the oppressed?

Anger is all of these, yet none of them. Anger is an inborn
emotion, and the natural response to frustration. Bruce W. Colburn, a clinical therapist at Riverside Psychiatric Institute in New-
port News, Virginia, calls anger "the psychological equivalent to
pain."[1] This is probably as good a definition as we can get. He also
calls it "a signal that things are not going right." This probably
should be corrected to read, "a signal that things are not going the
way we want."

Anyone who has ever spent much time in the company of an infant has seen anger in its simplest, most uncorrupted form. *What makes a baby angry?* Taking away his food before his appetite is satisfied. Putting him down when he wants to be held. Confining him when he wants to be free. Sticking him with a pin or a hypodermic needle. Failing to respond to his cries for company, food, or help.

Not every pain or frustration produces infantile anger, however. Fear seems to drive it out, and a great enough survival fear makes anger impossible. A baby threatened with being dropped from a height screams with terror, not anger. The same is true of an adult in immediate and deadly peril. Few people kept in concentration camps, or forced to undergo death marches, or subjected to daily beating and starvation tend to show much anger. They are too frightened, too demoralized.

So anger requires at least some sense of power in a situation, however small. The reason so many women suppress anger is that they feel so powerless. They are too afraid of abuse or abandonment to register anger.

So the social rebels are right. When a formerly cowed person begins to feel and show anger, this can be a hopeful sign. In her ground-breaking study, *Anger, The Misunderstood Emotion*, Carol Tavris argues that to respond to pain and provocation with anger is normal, whatever a person's age, sex, or class. Anger is part of our survival equipment. In a healthy personality, it expresses self-assertion and the will to live.

Unfortunately, not all personalities are healthy and not all anger is productive. The blind rage of rioters who burn down their neighbors' homes and leave innocent people without their shops, jobs, homes, and sometimes even their lives is not a liberating force. It is an oppressive one, as surely as the rage of the slave driver or abusive parent.

So, anger is natural and a sign of health, yet also dangerously destructive. It is universal to all, yet it has been permitted to some and denied to others. We're confused about it today because we are in an age of moral transition, where the old rules no longer apply but new ones have not yet been agreed upon.

How do we deal with the enormous force of generational anger, especially the anger of daughters against their fathers? The answer begins with the realization that it's not anger that's the problem but the way we express it.

Dealing with Anger

Angry daughters are sometimes hard to recognize because they fear confrontation. Instead, they may seek indirect outlets.

Anger can be dealt with in one of six ways:

- We can deny and suppress it.
- We can openly turn it on the person who displeases us.
- We can covertly turn it on the person who displeases us.
- We can turn it on ourselves.
- We can turn it on a third party.
- We can deal with the causes and consequences.

Denying and Suppressing Anger

Anger is like any other strong, spontaneous, natural emotion. However hard we may try to suppress it, if denied one outlet it will find another. Freud called this tendency the *Return of the Repressed,* and it is one of the most firmly established principles in psychology. A daughter who is too afraid of her father to express her anger directly may find covert ways of undermining him, or else take it out on safer targets, such as her mother or her siblings. Or she may try to be a saint and dam it up.

Dammed-up feelings build up dangerous pressures. Time and again, we hear about "nice guys, model citizens" who suddenly astound their neighbors with acts of murderous violence. And even where there is no such dramatic loss of control, repression is still destructive. The person who numbs her capacity for feeling anger may also numb her capacity for feeling love, for bonding, for compassion, for pleasure, and for joy, buying her relief at the price of feeling alive.

Openly Turning Anger on the Person Who Displeases Us

King Lear, as all-powerful king, punished anyone who defied his orders. Once his older daughters came to power, they did the same. In the end, both parties were destroyed.

Turning anger on a person less powerful than yourself is abuse. A father like Lear who victimizes his children when they are powerless may well find himself victimized in turn as the power passes into their hands. In our own day of declining living standards, disintegrating families, and widespread homelessness, *Lear* has a devastating immediacy. When the ruined old king huddles out in the rain with other homeless beggars—some psychotic, some diseased—we immediately recognize his circumstances. Many people are alone in the world because they have either abandoned their families or been abandoned by them, usually under the influence of anger.

According to therapist Bruce W. Colburn, chronically angry people like Lear, Goneril, and Regan have irrational expectations. They perceive those who displease them as doing the wrong thing or treating them badly. "What we have to do," Colburn says, "is get them to give up that notion. People don't always do what you want them to do. The world's not always fair. And behaving as if things were otherwise is a guaranteed losing struggle."[2]

The struggle is guaranteed to be lost because other people, unless terrorized into paralysis, naturally respond to provocation with resistance. They either strike back with their own anger, thus setting off an escalating power struggle, or they withdraw from the fray in disgust.

Covertly Turning Anger on Those Who Displease Us

Covert expressions of anger have the advantage of being too elusive for the victim to recognize them as an attack. Anorexia and bulimia are often expressions of hostility toward a parent, espe-cially a father. Self-starvation says to the parent, "I never could be thin enough or perfect enough to please you. Well, I'll show you how thin I can be. And you'll be so scared you won't dare to punish me."

Running away, living a life-style that the father detests, marrying the sort of man whom the father dislikes, making a poor appear-ance, not writing or phoning home for long periods, producing no grandchildren, or making other choices consciously or uncon-sciously calculated to cause distress may all be used effectively as covert attacks.

Covert attacks on the parent often seem to hurt the child as much or more than the parent, but that is almost incidental. In their perennial classic, *A New Guide to Rational Living*, Albert Ellis, Ph.D., and Robert A. Harper, Ph.D., explain why: Blame and pun-ishment, they point out, tend to boomerang. Other people are not so different from ourselves. Like us, they are the products of their upbringing and environment. Like us, they can occasionally do evil without being evil. Not only is it grandiose, therefore, to sit in judgment of them; the way we judge them also colors the way in which we judge ourselves.

> Lack of forgiveness toward others breeds lack of self-forgive-ness, with consequent perfectionistic attitudes toward your own failings and incompetencies. To devalue others because they have made some serious mistake helps you devalue the whole human race, including your own humanity.[3]

Turning Anger on Ourselves

Sometimes, even covert attacks on another seem impossible or dangerous. In that case, we may turn our anger on ourselves. Anger turned against the self can take many forms, including depression and stress-related disorders, such as colitis, ulcers, aller-gies, accident-proneness, menstrual difficulties, and a host of other illnesses.

Because of their physical and social disadvantages, women are particularly likely to deflect their anger away from its true targets and turn it on themselves. One form this takes is blaming themselves unfairly for other people's behavior. For this, they get plenty of social support. As Carol Tavris points out in *The Mismeasure of Woman,* the so-called Recovery and Co-Dependents' movements hold women responsible for "choosing" abusive or promiscuous men or for "enabling" men to be addicted. In fact, it's the patriarchal tradition that has given men permission to be abusive and promiscuous; and men are responsible for their own addictions.

Taking Anger Out on a Third Party

It's common for daughters who are angry at their fathers to divert their anger onto another target. Myra remembered being very happy until she was eleven, when her father, an attorney, left the family to marry one of his firm's young associates.

Myra excused her father by blaming his new wife for the breakup. For the next ten years, she was content to hate "that slut" and wait for her father to wake up to her worthlessness and come home again. Meanwhile, Myra grew up and married. Eventually, her father did leave his second wife, only to marry a third—a legal secretary little older than Myra. Rather than admit that her father was the type who trades in wives every decade or so, she again blamed the woman. When Myra's husband suggested that this newest bride was really a delightful person whom Myra might enjoy as a friend, she turned against him with such fury that they were soon on the verge of divorce.

Scapegoating third parties is an attempt to sacrifice a less-valued relationship in order to save the one that really matters. For reasons which Myra had never explored, her love for her father, or rather the ideal she clung to of her parents' marriage, meant more to her than anything else, including her own marriage.

134

Why Anger Can Be So Hard to Recognize

In old-fashioned romantic novels, the heroine often awakens on the last page to the realization that she has always loved the hero without knowing it. Modern readers may find this baffling. How can you love someone and not know it? But throughout much of history, women had to wait to be wooed and were laughed at if they showed a preference for a particular man. So they learned to censor their feelings.

Today, anger against the father is sometimes censored in the same way. Many daughters, like Myra, don't even know it's there. Some claim they merely "avoid" their fathers because they "have nothing in common," not realizing how angry they are. Others know that they are angry but seem angry out of proportion to the cause. This happens when the cause is an experience that happened so early that it could not be worked through at the time.

Dealing with the Causes and Consequences

Of all the six outlets for anger, confronting the causes and consequences of anger is the constructive one, and we will consider it closely in the second part of the book.

Nazis and Vampires

Poet Sylvia Plath is the voice of female rage against the father. Most of her best poems are driven by the monumental anger that she felt toward her father, who became fatally ill when she was six and died when she was eight.[4]

Otto Plath was past forty when Sylvia was born in 1932. A German immigrant and a college teacher, he is said to have adored his firstborn daughter but was somewhat strict. After he became ill, she had to tiptoe around the house and talk in whispers, which she resented fiercely.

135

His death left the family in financial difficulty. Sylvia's mother had no time to grieve but found a job immediately.

Yet Sylvia's feelings couldn't be kept buried. Like vampires, her grief and anger kept rising up to possess her. From the time she lost her father, some part of her always wanted to die, too. At nine, she had a nearly fatal accident. At twenty, she made a serious suicide attempt. At thirty, she finally killed herself.

Sylvia Plath was outstandingly gifted and attractive. She broke into print while still in high school and was a guest editor on *Mademoiselle* while still in college. After graduation, she won a fellowship to study in England, married into the British literary establishment, had two babies, published a novel and a volume of poetry, received excellent reviews, and was taken up by the media—all before the age of thirty.

Yet she was never happy for long. Her husband, poet Ted Hughes, was a few years older and enjoyed a wider reputation, so she felt in his shadow. She also resented having to look after the children while he devoted full time to his career. When she discovered that he was unfaithful, her early feelings of abandonment were triggered and she was overcome by grief and rage. Before taking her life, she poured her anguish into a volume of stunning, searing poems.

In the most famous, "Daddy," Sylvia identifies her father (through his German birth and accent) with the terrifying images of Germans prevalent during her wartime childhood. Her dead father became a Nazi and a vampire. Home was a concentration camp and Dracula's castle. She was a Jew, being tortured by Nazis and a peasant whose blood was feeding vampires. She also fuses her father and her husband: both vampires, both Nazis, one and the same.

"Daddy" ends as a revenge fantasy, in which she destroys both husband and father simultaneously with a stake through their one heart.

I was ten when they buried you.
At twenty I tried to die

And get back, back, back to you.
I thought even the bones would do.

But they pulled me out of the sack,
And they stuck me together with glue.
And then I knew what to do.
I made a model of you,
A man in black with a Meinkampf look

And a love of the rack and the screw.
And I said I do, I do. . . .

If I've killed one man, I've killed two—
The vampire who said he was you
And drank my blood for a year,
Seven years, if you want to know.
Daddy, you can lie back now.

There's a stake in your fat black heart
And the villagers never liked you.
They are dancing and stamping on you.
They always *knew* it was you.
Daddy, daddy, you bastard, I'm through [5]

Elizabeth Hardwick has called Plath's last poems "tirades . . . marked by destructiveness toward herself and others."[6] As a small child, Sylvia must have believed that her father had sickened and died in order to hurt her, and on some level she continued to believe it even as an adult. Apparently, even her children were more symbolic than real to her. She turned on the gas while they were in the house. Also, she literally did to them what she blamed her father for doing to her: she consciously abandoned them by dying.

Clearly, Sylvia Plath's husband and children suffered terribly for her anger at her father. So, at times, did her mother. But the one who suffered the most was Sylvia. Like Goneril and Regan, she nurtured her anger until it destroyed her.

137

Repeating the Past, Changing the Past

Unresolved conflicts from childhood tend to keep recurring through life, demanding solution. The main barrier to solution is that our childhood conflicts are so rooted in our childhood sub-personalities.

As children, few of us have much understanding of what is going on in the lives of our parents. Like Sylvia Plath, all we knew as children was how we were affected, how we felt. Today, when we compulsively repeat some reaction rooted in childhood, we often fall prey to emotions as blind, overpowering, and self-centered as a child's. We feel what we feel deeply, but we don't understand causes so we can't make changes.

Decisions

At the age of eight, Sylvia Plath apparently made a decision: *I'll stay angry until Daddy comes back from the dead.* Such decisions, made at an unconscious level, demand that the past be undone, fueling unhappiness.

The idea sounds absurd because it demands the impossible. Yet any time we blame our present misery on a past event, we are speaking out of a decision like Sylvia's. "It's all because *X* happened" translates into "I'll stay angry until *X* changes in the past." In other words, we make a decision not to give up our painful feelings until the resented event changes—as of course it never does.

Children aren't the only ones who make such decisions. Adults do it, too, although they make them with the most childlike parts of themselves. Every time something happens "too late," it's a good idea to suspect that a "decision" is involved. In F. Scott Fitzgerald's *The Beautiful and Damned,* the huge inheritance arrives "too late" for the thirty-something couple to enjoy it. They wanted to be rich when they were young! In *Gone With the Wind,* Scarlett discovers she loves Rhett "too late" to save the marriage. He wanted her love on his schedule, not hers.

Rationally, the "too-laters" know the past can't change. But the part of us that makes such decisions is not rational. When we make such a decision, we make changing the past a non-negotiable condition for giving up our misery and enjoying the present. Even when we are offered what we claim we want, we may turn away declaring, *Too late! Too late! I don't want it anymore! It's no good having it now if I couldn't have it then, when it mattered!*

"Too Late" Even for God

Sometimes even God Himself comes around "too late." In the 1991 film *The Rapture,* a depressed young woman named Sharon spends her days as an information operator, her nights chasing anonymous sex. In a moment of desperation, she is converted by a born-again sect that promises the end of the world in seven years. While waiting for "the Rapture" that will take the saved to Heaven, she marries, has a daughter, and is euphorically happy, until her husband's sudden death.

Refusing to grieve, relying on prophecy, Sharon abandons her home and possessions and takes her five-year-old into the desert to await the Rapture. As the days and weeks pass, she loses both her hope and her grip on reality. Finally, she and her starving, freezing child decide to give God "one more chance." When the Rapture fails to arrive by their deadline, Sharon shoots her daughter to put her out of her misery.

Then, miraculously, the Rapture *does* arrive, or perhaps it arrives only in Sharon's disintegrating mind. In either case, it's "too late" for her to forgive God. Sharon had loved Him conditionally, for as long as He made her happy and gave her what she demanded. When He gave her trials and troubles instead, she refused to love Him anymore. Now, even when He sends her little girl's spirit to fetch her to Heaven, she refuses to relent. She rejects Heaven on God's terms and chooses Hell.

God is the archetypal Father, and Sharon is the archetypal angry daughter. Unable to change the past retroactively, she would rather suffer eternally in bitter pride than to forgive God and be happy.

Silence

Anger can take many forms, including silence. Marsha, an early reader of this book, claimed not to be able to find herself among the six daughters. She had not spoken to her father, she said, since he hurt her mother with an affair several years before. Therefore, she believed, she didn't "have" a relationship at all.

Marsha claims that she does not speak to her father on moral grounds, because he caused her mother pain. Yet Marsha associates with other people who have been unfaithful to their spouses, probably causing them equal sorrow. Clearly, Marsha is not judging her father by the same standards by which she judges her friends. She sees him as a fallen idol rather than an ordinary, imperfect human being.

To an objective person, it's plain that Marsha is very, very angry. Her father is probably anguished, too, just as she intends him to be. Yet, for reasons that she has not explored, Marsha does not yet see that the desire to punish is always a product of anger.

Warring Father/Warring Daughter

The opposite of silence is constant, fierce quarreling. This pattern typically occurs between a father attempting to control his daughter and a daughter who refuses to be controlled. The daughter is often the more powerful party of the two, the father's anger being an expression of his frustration and fear of losing her, while the daughter's anger expresses her determination to run her own life. The daughter feels that she has less to lose than the father does because she is more willing to sacrifice the relationship.

Anger as a Defense against Victimization

Some daughters cultivate anger because it seems their only protection against exploitation. Only when they're very, very angry do they feel able to say *no.*

Linda, a forty-year-old client, had been the companion daughter of a Pygmalion father, Greg. She spent months in therapy before becoming willing to "divorce" him. Part of the "divorce" consisted of selling the mail-order business they had run together, which had been successful largely through her efforts.

Linda put her share of the profits into the down payment on a house that needed remodeling. Greg put his into a stock that was expected to rise but which fell instead. Six months after the company was sold, Greg asked Linda to lend him twenty-five thousand dollars to start up a new business, promising to repay her within the year. Linda had doubts about the ability of her seventy-three-year-old father to take on so much work alone, but felt unable to refuse him because he had done what she wanted about the mail-order company.

So Linda refinanced her house and gave Greg the money, never to see it again. As she had foreseen, his new business failed, leaving her with an overwhelming mortgage and a father who needed financial support as well.

Linda was furious at both her father and herself and wished she had gotten angry when he first came to her for the money. As she saw it, only anger would have given her the strength to say no. Yet there are other ways than through anger to avoid the victim's role. The patriarchal daughter's problem is that no one ever told her what they are.

Part Two

Part Two

8

THE DANCE OF THE MOTHER-RAISED CHILDREN

◆

[The] stone walls . . . have buried foundations.
—Dorothy Dinnerstein

How did the six father-daughter dances come about? What makes us still so susceptible to their drama? Can we really hope to overcome patterns that have been with us since childhood and with the human race for as long as people have been keeping records?

So far, we've been looking at these questions mainly from a social and historical point of view, observing how ancient ways of thinking perpetuate themselves. From now on, we'll be looking at fathers and daughters from a more inward, psychological, and personal angle. We'll be dealing with such questions as how traditional ways of thinking have conditioned our deepest feelings and most habitual behaviors, and what we can do to overcome their effects, both as individuals and as father-daughter pairs. We will also look at a model of what a truly loving father-daughter relationship could be like and how it might evolve over an entire shared lifetime.

The key is awareness. The less awareness we have, the more we remain programmed by social expectations and unconscious attitudes. The more awareness we have, the more alternatives and

145

possibilities we discover for ourselves and for our relationships. As Dorothy Dinnerstein observes in *The Mermaid and the Minotaur* "the quintessential feature of human life . . . is its self-creating nature."[1]

In this introductory chapter to part 2, we are going to be posing questions about how our experience as babies and children has shaped our adult attitudes. Some of these questions would have been totally unthinkable until very recent times. Some strike at such ingrained customs that they may sound crazy. For example: *How does it affect children to be raised by women, especially by their mothers?*

If the very question seems outrageous, it's no wonder. After all, who else is supposed to take care of children if not women, especially their mothers? Yet the fact that we take something for granted doesn't mean that it has no effect on us. On the contrary: the more prevalent a custom is, the more effect it has on us; and the less we're aware of the effect, the more powerful it becomes.

"Oh, that's just how it is. It's only natural," we tell ourselves. In fact, "it" may not be natural at all, merely something we're so used to that we can't imagine questioning it.

For example, we assume that a mother's care is all that a small baby needs, but is that true? We assume that fathers don't become important until later, but is that true? We assume that a man's primary satisfactions come from his work life, but is that true? We assume that it's healthy for school-age boys to reject their mothers and all females, but is that true? It used to be thought that Chinese and Swedes behaved differently from each other because they were born different; now we know that their differences are chiefly due to their different upbringing. To what extent is this also true about girls and boys?

What Is the Mother-Raised Child Theory?

Most modern psychological theories and therapies start from the assumption that infants and children pass through a sequence of developmental stages, and that they are strongly influenced at each stage by the treatment they receive from their caretakers. Even experiences that come too early to be consciously remembered leave permanent effects on the gut level. In fact, the earlier the experience, the more effect it may have, since it creates a context in which we interpret what comes later. According to the renowned child psychiatrist and theorist Erik Erikson, if we don't learn "basic trust" during our first few months of life, we are likely to carry a distrusting attitude throughout life.

Each stage builds on the foundation of the previous ones, and each is strongly affected by our mental and emotional maturity at the time. This means that even the most mature among us are still strongly influenced by impressions formed at the age of a few months or a few years.

When Freud first suggested this theory, it struck many as preposterous. Yet today it is widely accepted. How else could we even begin to understand why a healthy, beautiful young woman like Sylvia Plath, with two beloved babies and a promising career, would kill herself over the breakup of her marriage? Her action only makes sense once we realize that losing her husband reactivated her childhood response to the loss of her father.

But while Freud addressed many questions that had never been asked before, he left many others unasked. Very much a man of his time, he took the customs of nineteenth-century Vienna for granted. He accepted as a *given* that males and females are profoundly different, that males are superior, that women should devote their lives to child raising, and that men should be remote from it. It never occurred to him that such a system of child raising might be a vicious circle.

The *Mother-Raised Child* theorists rethink Freud's *given*. They also rethink Freud in another way. Freud emphasized the impact of *trauma*—shocking, nonroutine events—on child development, giving little thought to the shaping effects of daily life. *Mother-Raised Child* theorists, in contrast, focus attention on the impressions laid down and reinforced on a daily basis in the minds of

147

young children who are raised by women and see little of men. They offer a way of understanding not only *how* boys and girls turn out as they do, but *why.*

Some key books in the field are Dorothy Dinnerstein's *The Mermaid and the Minotaur,* Nancy Chodorow's *The Reproduction of Mothering,* and Lillian B. Rubin's *Intimate Strangers.* We will draw freely on their observations, adding our own.

How Does the Mother-Raised Child Theory Describe Infancy?

When the father is remote and the mother (or some other woman) is always there, the infant has a very different experience of the two sexes. The whole world seems to consist of the mother— and a very confusing, unpredictable world it is. Mother provides nourishment, but not always right away. She sings lullabies, then leaves the room. She's the one who says *I love you,* but also *No.* She comforts and caresses, yet also scolds and later demands bowel and bladder control. The baby has no notion of her motives. She's not perceived as a person with a life and needs, but as an all-powerful yet arbitrary force.

Inevitably, the baby develops some very ambivalent feelings toward this force: love and trust and dependency and possessiveness on the one hand; disappointment, resentment, and rage on the other. No mother, not even the most attentive on earth, could spare her child this conflict, because no mother can provide a totally painless and satisfying world. Besides, the child *needs* to struggle with the environment in order to achieve a separate identity and will.

How Does the Mother-Raised Child See Women?

The mother is the baby's source of both pleasure and pain. Whatever goes right is her gift. Whatever goes wrong is her fault. Eventually, the child discovers that Mama is a woman and assumes that other women must be like Mama. If she is all-powerful, wonderful, terrible, and incomprehensible, so must all women be.

According to Dorothy Dinnerstein, women come to be seen as *dirty goddesses:* kind and cruel, giving and withholding, desirable and treacherous, loved and feared.[2] This perception of mother and woman is imprinted in the rock-bottom, gut-level stratum of the mother-raised infant's mind—prerationally, preconsciously, preverbally, and therefore very hard to question or uproot.

How Does the Mother-Raised Child See Men?

If fathers played a major role in child raising, much of the baby's ambivalence would be directed at them. As it is, by remaining remote, the father stays pure in the baby's eyes. As he emerges from the background of things that are "not Mother," his relatively rare appearances are perceived as special occasions. Because he takes little part in the frustrations of the child's daily life, he is not resented. In time, the child learns that the father spends his time in a larger world outside of the nursery, and this gives him prestige.

Inevitably, the father is perceived as very different from the mother. He's the first individual that the child gets to know *as* an individual, rather than as an all-pervading presence. Since he's also the first *man* the child gets to know, he comes to represent all men, just as the mother represents all women. So the mother-raised child tends to see the father as a symbol of individuality and independence, an alternative to the mother and a refuge from her, the model for building a separate, grown-up identity.

Not surprisingly, mother-raised children idolize the father, and this idolization is set down early enough that it still seems gut level. The small child needs a model of independence and individuality. If no actual father is available, the child will manufacture one out of the male images in fairy stories and the media, or out on the street.

These early impressions solidify during the toddler stage. As Dr. Lillian Rubin explains, the toddler is still a profoundly dependent creature who needs protection and wants to be taught. Yet during toddlerhood resistance to the mother becomes strong. Most toddlers are far more willing to "behave" for their fathers than their mothers, and this tendency usually goes on throughout childhood. In fact, many people carry this two-year-old's attitude into adult life as well, respecting male bosses and resenting female ones.

It's amazing how short a time ago it was that everyone took this attitude for granted. A 1971 episode of *Columbo* was recently revived as a TV special. At one point, the kindly detective questions a young man with a woman employer. "How can you do it?" he asks. "I mean, how can you work for a woman?" Columbo would know better than to ask such a question today.

How Does Mother-Raising Encourage the Low Status of Women?

It seems so unfair. The mother is resented because she gives the child so much, whereas the father is prized because he gives so little. Yet it makes emotional sense.

Some adopted children discount the people who have put in the effort of raising them, while idealizing the birth parents who gave them away. Yet we can understand that, too, just as we can understand why married people may dream of lost sweethearts or lust after movie stars or idolize the lovers whom they meet for brief, stolen hours. We only get hungry for what we don't have and idealize people whom we don't really know.

As Emily Dickinson wrote:

Success is counted sweetest
By those who ne'er succeed—
To comprehend a nectar
Requires sorest need.

So underfathered children go on yearning for their fantasy fathers, while their devoted mothers bear the burden of all the children's dissatisfactions and resentments. And when the children

150

grow up, they carry those same attitudes with them, with the result that men, in general, tend to be overvalued and women to be underappreciated.

How Soon Can a Baby Tell the Difference Between Mother and Father?

Is all this just a theory? Can infants tell whether a man or a woman is handling them? And does it matter?

Some surprising answers to these questions have surfaced in the last couple of years.

Under a five-year grant from the National Institute of Health, developmental psychologist Sandra Weiss of the University of California at San Francisco has been studying the effect of touch on babies and children.[3] Her research confirms that touch is the primary sense in newborns and remains powerfully important throughout childhood. Touch stimulates the development of intelligence, emotional responsiveness, self-concept, self-esteem, and body image.

Her evidence shows that even newborns respond very differently to physical handling by men and women. Men typically use a "more intense and stimulating" touch, which appears to "provide critical sensory feedback."[4] In fact, a man's touch may be downright dangerous for premature and other high-risk infants since it increases the heart rate and raises the blood pressure. But healthy babies thrive on it.

Sandra Weiss is convinced that contact with the father is significant from birth and that, contrary to what was believed in the past, "We cannot assume that the mother-child relationship is the primary influence during the child's early years."[5]

T. Berry Brazelton, the distinguished pediatrician and author, has recently identified three kinds of loving parental touch:

1. Gentle petting, which calms the child and promotes sleep.
2. More intense petting, which alerts the child and promotes wakefulness and attention.

3. Exciting, playful touch, which stimulates the child and encourages physical alertness and movement.[6]

This third kind of touch is the one that Sandra Weiss has found
to be associated with handling by men.

Pediatricians Tiffany Field, director of the Touch Research Institute, and Ed Tronick, director of the Child Development Unit at
Children's Hospital in Boston, have associated lack of touching
with growth delays. Both experts are concerned with the effect on
the development of daughters by a lack of physical contact with
their fathers.[7]

So it seems that children have a built-in need for hands-on care
by both sexes, and that our traditional system of leaving them
mostly in the care of women has had wide-ranging and detrimental
effects. Up to now, we have assumed that these effects were simply
human nature, whereas they are actually the result of mother-
raising.

What Happens to Mother-Raised Girls?

It's during toddlerhood that children first come to understand
which sex they are. The girl learns that she will someday become
a woman, like her mother. For many, this appears to be a wonderful discovery. They are thrilled to realize that they will someday
have babies of their own and acquire something like their mother's
magic.

One result is that girls tend to remain close to their mothers,
absorbing lessons in how to be warm, nurturing, and intimate. Yet
even while the little girl identifies with her mother, she may go on
resenting her dominance and unpredictability and also compete
with her for the father's attention. The result can be a lifelong
love-hate relationship.

At the same time, mother-raised girls see less than they want to
of their fathers. As a result, they may overvalue, submit to, and
court the attention of men. Not all mother-raised daughters follow

this pattern, but those who do are set up for stereotyped "feminine" behavior.

What Happens to Mother-Raised Boys?

When a mother-raised toddler boy realizes that he is destined to become a man, he starts looking to his father for a model. If what he sees is someone remote, independent, and undemonstrative, sometimes even domineering or violent, he concludes that this is how men are supposed to be. In the effort to become more like his father, he must become less like his mother, which means giving up his closeness to her. This goal is supposed to be achieved by the time he enters school. The schoolboy who is still "tied to his mother's apron strings" is thought to have something seriously the matter with him.

The boy's flight from the feminine takes place on a level of consciousness in which gut-level feelings are combined with verbalized slogans, such as "Big boys don't cry," and "She's only a girl."

Typically, a boy's friendships are based on shared interests and activities, rather than emotional intimacy. It may even seem that the growing boy loses his capacity for deep feeling. What actually happens is that his emotions remain powerful but are diverted to outlets safely removed from the supposedly feminine world of personal relationships. Spectator sports, for example, allow otherwise impassive men to express passionate joy and sorrow over the results of a ball game. Politics provide a similar outlet, encouraging exultation or despair over the results of elections. Fanatic devotion to one's country, race, religion, ancestors, clan, ethnic group, neighborhood, language, culture, work, heroes, or leaders are also approved substitutes for the forbidden love of mother.

Because these passions are so powerful in a man's life, they seem entirely natural. Yet they are far more a matter of custom than nature. It costs a little boy dearly to give up his first and greatest love, even if the void does get filled partially by the Red Sox, the

Motherland, or Der Führer. When puberty arrives, forcing him to seek women again, he finds his soul in conflict.

This conflict is the source of male terror described by Wolfgang Lederer in *The Fear of Women.* The yearning to surrender to some woman's embrace is opposed by everything he went through at six. Theoretically, the emotionally healthy man will one day be able to love a woman of his own as devotedly as he once loved his mother. Yet it doesn't often happen that way. Instead, many men feel unable to approach a woman without those feelings of wariness and contempt, of smothering and threat, that became a part of him in childhood.

No wonder some men prefer to buy sex from women they despise than to risk loving one woman. No wonder pornography aimed at men divorces sex from emotion and links it to power. The adult mother-raised boy associates women and emotion and attempts to control them both. This impulse comes not from strength, as he likes to believe, but from fear—the fear that if he doesn't control them, they'll control him. For this same reason, control becomes a central issue in men's lives: control not only over women and feelings, but also over nature, events, and other men.

Mother-raised boys identify with their father's remoteness, which they idealize as manly strength and reason. They attempt to control their emotions, which they associate with womanly weakness and irrationality. Not all mother-raised sons follow this pattern, but those who do are set up for stereotyped "masculine" behavior.

Is the Need Mutual? Does the Father Need the Child as Well?

During the seventies and eighties, a variety of studies established that marriage benefits men more than it benefits women, that married men outlive single men and that widowed men sicken and die faster than widowed women. These were "counter-intuitive" results—that is, contrary to the popular notions that most men want to be free and that women have to lure them into the "tender trap."

Now, somewhat similar results are showing up in preliminary studies about fatherhood. In a 1991 Wellesley College study headed by researcher Rosalind Barnet, it was found that men who had close relationships with their children enjoyed better mental and physical health and less job stress than men who either did not have children or were not actively involved with their raising.[8]

So, just as contact with the father is "good for" the baby, contact with the baby is apparently "good for" the father, too. If this is so, then the fathers of father-starved children are themselves child starved. They need the contact just as much as the child does, but because they have learned to suppress that need, they perpetuate more generations of mutual starvation.

What we are learning implies that women may have to accept men as equals in the nursery. If so, they may not find it easy. Just as many men assume that they have a special expertise in the workplace, many women assume that they have it at home. In *The Second Shift*, social psychologist Arlie Hochschild gives examples of husbands who fail to "help" their working wives with child care.[9] In at least a couple of cases, the wives saw themselves as the boss at home and tried to assign chores to their husbands, with the result that the husbands became resentful and less cooperative than ever.

What Happens When Children Are Raised by Nurses?

According to the Mother-Raised Child theory, the abandonment of children to their mothers is not healthy but harmful, and the character types that it produces are not natural but distorted. But what happens when children are raised by nurses instead of mothers? How do they feel about their mothers? How do they feel about their nurses?

In many societies where children are raised by nurses, the mothers are almost as remote as the fathers and are treated with almost equal formality and respect. Predictably, having two distant parents instead of one tends to mean that both will be idealized.

In the early Renaissance, when upper-class newborns were handed over to wet nurses, poets like Dante and Petrarch wrote magnificent love poems for noble ladies whom they had merely glimpsed from afar, and knights devoted their deeds to women of superior station. Perhaps what these men were expressing was the yearning that they had felt as babies for the mothers who were strangers to them.

At the same time, such arrangements tended to foster arrogance in the upper class and a rigid caste system throughout society. Seldom has violence been more casual, continual, and brutal than in the Italy of Dante and Petrarch. Highborn ladies might have been celebrated in song, but ordinary women, of the class of nurses, were despised.

Closer to home, a similar situation arose in the American South. Both before and after the Civil War, any white woman who could afford it turned child care over to a black "mammy." Not surprisingly, this society also made an enormous distinction between the reserved and haughty "ladies," who were placed on pedestals, and the despised "wenches" of the black and "poor white trash" categories.

In her novel and play, *The Member of the Wedding,* set in the Deep South during the 1940s, Carson McCullers explores the relationship between Frankie, a motherless white preteen girl with a neglectful father, and the wise and kindly black nurse who has raised her. Child and nurse share a great intimacy, marked by mutual understanding and compassion. But when Frankie, at twelve, is befriended by a popular white girl and invited to join an exclusive club, she becomes contemptuous of the nurse, signaling that the relationship is over.

In her 1961 autobiography, *Killers of the Dream,* Southern novelist Lillian Smith described a similar event in her own childhood, and the guilt and shame associated with the sacrifice:

I knew that my old nurse who had cared for me . . . who soothed me, fed me, delighted me with her stories and games, let me fall asleep on her warm, deep breast, was not worthy of the passionate love I felt for her but must be given instead a half-smiled-at affection. I knew . . . that the deep respect I felt for her, the tenderness, the love, was a childish thing which every normal child outgrows . . . and that somehow—though it seemed impossible to my agonized heart—I too must out-grow these feelings. . . . I learned to cheapen with tears and sentimental talk of "my old mammy" one of the profound relationships of my life.[10]

Substitute *mother* for *nurse* and *mammy,* and *boy* for *child,* and you have the ordeal of every mother-raised boy, who must sacrifice his mother to claim his superior social status. By the time Lillian Smith wrote *Killers of the Dream,* there was a growing consensus that racism was wrong. Perhaps the reason we do not yet have similar confessions from men about their repudiations of their mothers is that this manifestation of sexism is still believed to be normal and necessary.

Repudiating the mother who bore you must be even more trau-matic than repudiating your nurse, however beloved. Yet the pres-sure on the male child is unrelenting. Soon after he starts school, he learns to dread being perceived as a "Mama's Boy," yet a girl of twice that age can still take pride in being her "Daddy's Girl." This difference arises from the fact that the male belongs to the socially superior gender.

What Happens When Mothers Work?

Preparing to write *Childhood's Future,* Richard Louv traveled around the U.S. interviewing parents, teachers, children, and teens. He found that today's young people whose mothers have left home to work tend to be pathetically lonely, adrift, fearful, and poorly educated, yet, paradoxically, "surprisingly compassionate

157

toward their parents and their parents' generation." Typically, they expressed deep admiration and understanding:

> "You *have* to respect your parents. My father, he was smuggled from Puerto Rico to Miami when he was thirteen . . . but now he's a district attorney in New York."

> "You know how when you're young, you wonder, Why she want to make me do that? I can't stand her. As you grow older, you understand they're just trying to protect you."

> "It's gotten to the point where the field my dad's in, you're not always sure you're going to have a job tomorrow 'cause they're laying off and on, so we have to save."[11]

The children who express such feelings, says Louv, have been "thrown into battle alongside their parents" and feel comradely toward them. He contrasts their respectful admiration with "the lack of empathy that many baby boomers had for their parents' generation."[12] Baby boomers, those born roughly between 1945 and 1960, had been raised under what were thought to be ideal circumstances, by care-giving mothers and wage-earning fathers, in relative affluence, often in new, clean, safe suburbs, yet they grew up to resent their elders. Apparently, "ideal circumstances" don't always produce love or happiness.

Does all this mean that both mothers and fathers should keep their distance from their children, in order to get their respect? Certainly not. Parental distance causes its own problems. What the Mother-Raised Child theory indicates is the need of the child to receive plenty of hands-on care and training from both parents, to be exposed early and habitually to both sexes. In this way, ambivalence will not be mainly directed toward one sex and idealization toward the other, but a more realistic and balanced concept of both may be achieved.

What this line of thinking also indicates is that we are astonishingly ignorant of how children develop and what their human potential is. For thousands of years, the patriarchal family system of mother-taking-care-of-baby and father-taking-care-of-the-world has been producing women and men beautifully adapted to their roles. But it has achieved this only by starving children of their fathers and overexposing them to their mothers, thus creating handicaps for both sexes.

How Can We Know That Both Boys and Girls Are Handicapped?

Mother-raised boys and girls develop different values and abilities. In *In a Different Voice*, Carol Gilligan demonstrates the effect on the moral sense.[13] For boys, she says, moral ideas are related to reciprocity and the fulfillment of obligations, rather than cooperation or offering help. For girls, morality is a matter of doing good and not causing harm. In short, boys ask whether a choice is right or wrong, girls whether it will help or hurt.

Gilligan shows how male bias in favor of male values prejudiced a study based on the work of Lawrence Kohlberg.[14] Sixth graders were asked to resolve a dilemma: *A man has a dying wife who can be saved by an expensive drug, which he is too poor to buy. Is it better for him to steal the drug or to let his wife die?*

The reasoning of one particular boy and girl were closely studied as being typical. The boy instantly decided that the man should steal the drug, since a life is worth more than money. The girl considered other alternatives, such as negotiating with the druggist or borrowing. She questioned the druggist's right to withhold the medicine and the justice of allowing a woman to die because she is poor.

The researcher saw the girl's approach as immature, indicating an inability to stick to the point. As Gilligan observes, he failed to recognize it as a quest for a more satisfactory solution.

The boy's thinking had great strengths and also great weaknesses. It was focused and logical, quickly arriving at a decision that was both clear and humane. Yet it was also simplistic and even impractical, since acting on it would probably land the man in prison.

The girl's strength was her capacity to break the set, to step outside the either-or formulation, a capacity associated with high creativity. Her weakness was her failure to establish priorities or produce a plan of action. The theoretical wife could have died while she was still ruminating.

Which, then, is the superior mode of intelligence—the boy's logical, focused, but narrow approach, or the girl's meandering but comprehensive one?

Obviously, each has its drawbacks. An ideal mind would be both focused *and* comprehensive, logical *and* creative. An ideal society would respect both modes—logic leading to decision and action, as well as thoughtfulness, practicality, and concern for consequences. But mother-raised children, apparently, have trouble putting the two sets of abilities together.

Gilligan also illustrates how threatened some men feel by intimate situations.[15] Shown a picture of a man and woman seated on a bench by a river and asked to come up with a story, 20 percent of the males produced scenarios featuring danger, violence, and treachery—such as the couple watching the woman's husband drown, so that they could collect his insurance. In contrast, the women associated intimacy with happiness and came up with pleasant scenarios.

The Mother-Raised Father and the Mother-Raised Daughter

The six father-daughter patterns that have evolved and persisted through the centuries are at least in part the social consequence of both fathers and daughters being mother-raised:

Lost Father/Yearning Daughter:
Here, the father keeps his distance or even runs away, out of his stunted capacity for intimacy and his gut-level conviction that his

160

manhood requires him to repudiate women. The daughter, meanwhile, is driven by her unsatisfied hunger for father-contact, intensified by idealization, often dooming her to live in a dreamworld.

Abusive Father/ Victim Daughter:

The abusive father acts on the conviction that he must exercise total control over his females, or else cease to be a man. The victim daughter is at his mercy, partially because of her slighter size and strength but also due to her hunger for contact—any contact—and her tendency to blame herself so that she can continue to idealize him.

Pampering Father/ Spoiled Daughter:

The indulgent father divides and conquers, exercising power over the daughter by being bountiful, and over the daughter's mother by winning the daughter away. The spoiled daughter gets her father-hunger satisfied while triumphing over her mother, who carries all the responsibility for socializing the child, and therefore all the child's resentment.

Pygmalion Father/ Companion Daughter:

The Pygmalion father takes advantage of the daughter's resentment of her mother and idealization of himself to shape her to be the companion he desires. The daughter's resentment of her mother, along with her overvaluation of her father, make the process easy.

Ruined Father/ Rescuing Daughter:

The man who has struggled all his life to maintain his masculine superiority may be only too grateful to put himself into his daughter's care, once illness or age gives him an excuse. The daughter who struggled in vain to woo her father may be only too grateful to let him play baby so that she can play mother.

Anguished Father/ Angry Daughter:

The abusive or abandoning father who may want to sink back into babyhood may come up against a daughter too angry to play the

161

loving mother and only too eager to play the punishing one. Such a daughter has achieved the same separation from the father that the father once made from his own mother, suppressing the capacity for human mutuality with the opposite sex, and substituting the destructive desire for control.

Can We Break the Cycle?

Dancing these old patriarchal dances benefits neither partner. The good news is, there is no need to keep on dancing them. We can break the cycle and learn new steps—either in willing partnership with our fathers or daughters, or else alone.

9

SOLO DANCES

◆

You release yourself today from yesterday's
scenario. You work in tomorrow, guilt gone.

—Lewis Smedes, *Forgive and Forget*[1]

The Disappointing Father

What if you're alone in your quest to right the wrongs of the
past? What if your father or daughter is dead or won't talk to you
or if all your attempts to make things better end in frustration?

In Mona Simpson's novel, *The Lost Father*, Ann Stevenson, who
also calls herself Mayan, drops out of medical school to search for
the father who abandoned her in childhood. Mayan can't trust and
can't love and is convinced that nothing will cure her but finding
her father.

Her search takes her across America, to Egypt and back again,
leaving her drowning in debt. Then, at last, she does find him, and
what is he? A fifty-five-year-old restaurant manager, living with a
silly wife in a shabby rental in a colorless small city in the Central
Valley of California.

When she appears at his door, his response is all she could have
hoped. "I told him, because he did not know, 'I am your daughter,'
and then everything turned different, he was jumping and yelling,
he pulled me in waltzing, crying over my hand."[2]

163

But the euphoria soon fades. Mayan presses him for explanations. *Why did he leave?* Well, he and her mother didn't get along. *Why had he never sent money?* Well, he was usually broke. *Why had he never tried to find her?* Well, he intended to—"someday." Mayan wants compensation for the past. For her birthday, she asks for a genuine pearl necklace costly enough to make up for all the presents that she never got, but he sets a five-hundred-dollar limit and that won't buy real pearls.

So, finding her father solves no mysteries, performs no miracles. "Why you are unwanted: that is the only question. . . . But there is no answer. Never. He does not know. . . . He was only a man with his own troubles who didn't manage to keep track of his wife and child . . . He was only a man."[3]

Yet from this disappointment comes healing. If he's "only a man," what's there to do but make peace with the poor wretch that he is and get on with her own life? He can be in that life, but at the periphery, not the center. When he invites her for a week's vacation, she finds she can only give him two days.

"I had to find him to stop waiting," she realizes. "So long as you look for them, you're looking in the wrong place. I'm still looking, but not there."[4]

The Disappointing Daughter

In the fine film *Mississippi Masala,* a father makes a similar discovery. Of Indian descent, he and his family are forced out of Uganda, the land of their birth, when Idi Amin expels all Asians in 1972. They finally end up in Mississippi.

The father spends the next twenty years obstinately petitioning the Ugandan government to give him back his citizenship and property. At last, incredibly, he gets a response. His presence in Uganda is requested. A hearing has been arranged.

The only child of the family is a daughter, Mina, now in her mid-twenties. Back in Uganda, Mina had been a pampered princess, living in a gorgeous mansion, waited on by black servants. Now, she cleans toilets in a motel. Her father still sees her as a princess. She sees herself as a Mississippi "darky." When she falls in love with an African-American, the father is appalled and struggles to keep the lovers apart.

He flies off to Uganda as to his last hope. But when he arrives, he finds everything changed beyond recognition. His mansion is a ruin, his best friend is dead, and there is no role for people like himself. At last, he understands that the past is irretrievable and that all he has is the present. When he takes a black Ugandan child into his arms, he symbolically embraces his own future grandchildren. Heading back to Mississippi, he writes to his wife, "Home is where the heart is and my heart is with you."

Changing the Past and Redecision Therapy

The daughter in *The Lost Father* and the father in *Mississippi Masala* are committed to the belief that someday, somehow, if only they are willing to suffer long and hard enough, the past will be undone and they will get back what they have lost. This is the dream that Gloria Vanderbilt thought had come true when she became engaged to Leopold Stokowski: "Soon, very soon now, everything that happened long ago—all the ugliness—will be erased."

A tremendous amount of human suffering stems from the indulgence in this one magical belief: *If only I suffer long enough, what was wrong will be made right in the past.* This is an idea that comes right out of infancy: *If only I get hungry enough and cry long enough, I will be picked up and fed.*

Consciously, we all know the past can't be changed. Unconsciously, we may go on acting as if it could be. Mayan Stevenson in *The Lost Father* is acting according to the decision: *If I suffer and search for my father long enough, he will love me and provide me with what I needed from him in the past.* Every long-term grudge we carry, every obsession with a long-past injustice or sorrow, every angry quarrel with the absent or dead is based on the conviction that we can get what we never had if only we don't give up.

The decisions we make under the influence of this belief determine our perceptions of ourselves, our relations with others, and the options that we permit ourselves. They also put us on emotional treadmills. To get off, we first have somehow to get it through our heads that the treadmill will take us nowhere no matter how long we stay on. Then we have to find a path that does lead somewhere. One way to do that is through a process known as *Redecision Therapy*, which we will be describing shortly.

The Lost Father and *Mississippi Masala* are virtual casebook illustrations of the redecision process. In these stories, events force the central characters to confront their fantasies and see how unrealistic they always were. By letting go of the past, they inherit the present and the future. They trade in anger for forgiveness, resentment for gratitude, turmoil for peace.

For most of us, enlightenment may not come in as neat a package as it does in books or movies. Even so, we all have the capacity to become conscious of our fantasy-based decisions, then to make redecisions that will promote happiness, not ruin it.

The Insatiable Woman and the Disapproving Man

Mariel was a charming woman in her forties, once divorced and once widowed, who ran a modestly successful literary agency and had little trouble attracting men. She had entered group therapy, she said, because she wanted to "stop choosing men who keep threatening to disappear."

Her first husband, the one she divorced, had been chronically unfaithful. Her second had died of a sudden heart attack after just a few happy years. Her present lover, Jay, had been entangled in a protracted divorce for as long as she had known him. He was a scintillating man and their relationship was mostly a joy, yet from time to time, out of the blue, Jay would announce, "We're getting too intense. I've got to back off. I don't want to jump from one marriage directly into another."

Each time this happened, Mariel would suffer intensely. If only she were five pounds thinner or five years younger or had a different manner or voice, she told herself, he wouldn't be rejecting her.

She would beg Jay to tell her what she'd done or what was missing in their relationship, but he had no answer and would soon be behaving as if the explosion had never taken place.

The late Dr. Robert Goulding, coauthor of *Changing Lives through Redecision Therapy,* worked with Mariel to change her reaction to Jay.[5] He asked her to describe a time from her childhood when her father had said, in effect, "You are too intense. I need to back off."

"That's easy," said Mariel. "My father always said I was *insatiable.* Is that the same?"

"Sounds like it to me. What's the scene?"

"Well, we are walking in the park. I'm just a kid. He's telling me about when I was a baby. I threw a toy out of my crib, he says. He picked it up and threw it back, and I threw it out again. He says he kept this up to see how long I'd go on, to see how insatiable I was. 'You wouldn't ever quit,' he says, sounding totally disgusted with me."

"Go on," Bob prompted.

"Growing up, whenever I asked for something, he would say, 'You're just insatiable.' When I'm in a relationship, I still feel I must ask for nothing and give everything. Otherwise, I'll be exposed for the insatiable monster I am. But at the same time, I always feel that whatever I do is not enough. I'm trapped."

"Then admit to yourself that you are insatiable," Bob suggested. "Put your father in that chair and tell him, 'I'm insatiable and I'm proud of it!' "

"But I'm not proud of being insatiable!" Mariel protested. "If that's what I am, I hate it."

"It's time you learned to be proud of being insatiable," Bob told her. "Your father manipulated you into thinking you were a monster for having desires, because he was afraid of having to satisfy them—or was too self-absorbed to give easily to his lovely daughter. Test out saying, " 'I'm proud to be insatiable.' "

Mariel was still incredulous. "But why would I be proud?"

"Imagine you're a little girl who loves to play catch with her father," Bob said. "She throws a toy and he throws it back, and she loves the game. When she's a little older, she walks with him and wants his company as often as she can get it. Be proud."

Mariel's face brightened. "Oh! I'm proud because that means I have wants that are okay. And it means I know what I want."

"You got it. Say more," said Bob with a smile.

"I'm insatiable and I'm proud of it. I'm curious. I want love. I have yearnings. I love to play with a man. Yes, those are the best parts of me. I never thought of it—thought of myself—in such a positive way. I am insatiable and I'm proud of it. And I'm looking for a man who is curious too and has wants and wants love and who isn't afraid of my wants and loves to play with me."

"Now send your father away," said Bob, "and put Jay on the chair. Tell him."

"Jay, I am not a monster," Mariel declared. "I am loving and enthusiastic and I'm looking for a man who is not afraid of my wants. I'm insatiable and proud of it, and I'm looking for a man who loves me and wants me to play and play."

"Now be Jay," said Bob, "and answer for him."

Mariel moved to Jay's chair, "I love your enthusiasm, Mariel. I love the way you give to me. Sometimes you want more relationship that I'm ready for, but that doesn't make either of us monsters. I like your being insatiable, and I don't think I want you to change anything about yourself. Just know that sometimes I'll be needing to back off for a bit."

Mariel returned to her own chair and responded without prompting. "Jay, you're right." She then burst out laughing and bowed to the applause of the group.

Asked how she felt, she said, "Ten pounds lighter and twenty years younger." After some months of practicing this new way of thinking, she no longer felt burdened by the shame that her father had taught her.

Why Redecision Therapy Works

Redecision therapy liberates us from the repetition compulsion by taking us back in time to the period when a decision was made, bringing it to consciousness, putting it to a reality test, then enabling us to make a more appropriate decision in the here and now.

As children, we lived in worlds of fantasy. The people close to us loomed enormous and seemed to have wondrous powers. Our mothers were queens and fairy godmothers when they satisfied our wishes, wicked witches when they didn't. Our fathers were kings or giants. We also had no idea of the limits of our own powers. We thought we could make things happen by wishing, so when things went wrong, we found it easy to believe it was our own fault.

Our caretakers instinctively knew what our mental world was like and entertained us with stories about fantastical beings, last-minute rescues, long sufferings rewarded, wishes that came true, and happy endings. As we grew up and learned about cause-and-effect, we discovered that the magic world of our childhood was not "real" and that only "superstitious" or "primitive" or "unscientific" adults believed in it. Yet, on an unconscious level, we continued to believe.

The early decisions that we made were rooted in magical thinking. Picture a child constantly betrayed by a father who makes promises he doesn't keep. The child we're imagining is only three or four or five years old. Her father can't be "just a man" to her because she has no idea of what "just a man" is. Instead, he's a god, a king, a giant, the whole male sex, a major power in the universe. If she can't trust him, how can she trust God or life or any man?

But living in a world that can't be trusted is too scary to bear. Even Einstein once remarked that the most important question about the universe is "Is the world a safe place?" Because the young child still believes in magic, she supposes that it's within her power to change her father. So she wishes and prays and tries this and that behavior and still nothing works. Yet she goes on trying, because—on an unconscious level—she has a fixed idea that having a safe world to live in requires changing her father.

Months pass and years pass. The child is ten, twenty, forty. She looks back on the past with fury. By not keeping his promises, her father ruined her life! Perhaps she attends "adult child" support groups, exchanging sympathy with other "abuse survivors." In *The Mismeasure of Woman*, social psychologist Carol Tavris points out how recovery and codependency "support" groups sometimes encourage members to see themselves as irreparably damaged, lifelong victims who can never really recover from the past.[6] It is axiomatic among such groups that complete "recovery" is impossible because it would require the past to be undone, the abuse never to have happened.

A Redecision therapist would see it very differently: the "survivor's" problem is not so much the occurrence of the abuse as the decisions that were made around it. The father fails to keep a promise and the child decides, *I'm never going to trust anyone until Daddy goes back and keeps his promises.* This sort of decision depends on a magical belief: *If I'm willing to suffer long enough, what I wanted will happen.* Even after the adult consciously gives up that hope, her child subpersonality may still go on believing that there can be no really happy ending without it.

One technique used by Redecision therapists is to ask a client to state how many more months or years she is willing to go on suffering. "Ten years? Five years? One year? One month? How much would be appropriate?" One client was asked to say to the "father" in the empty chair, "Daddy, I'm only going to give you ten more years to learn to love me." Hearing herself, she was convulsed with laughter.

Until asked to set a time limit, most clients don't realize that they have any choice about their suffering. Liberation comes with the realization that it's not the past that controls us but our decisions about the past, and that it's within our power to decide whether to be victims or not.

Objections to Redecision Therapy

Perhaps you believe that letting go of the past is a sellout, that it exonerates those who hurt you and lets them off the hook. Actually, the person who gets off the hook is you. Your long-dead father is not hurt by your bitterness. Your daughter living on the opposite coast is not punished by your pain.

Or perhaps you fear what would become of you without your anger, rage, grief, or frustration. This is a reasonable fear. As short-term responses to recent events, such feelings warn us that something is wrong and prod us to make changes. But when they become linked to long-term suffering over events of years ago, they become the opposite of useful. Instead of stimulating a change for the better, they bind us to a harmful situation.

Or perhaps your misery has come to seem inevitable, and even a source of pride. "Anyone who'd been through what I've been through would feel the same way," you may think. Such a protest can be translated back into the original decision: *I'm going to go on suffering until X changes in the past.*

If Only . . .

The intention to remain miserable until some magical event takes place is often expressed by *if only*. *If only* my mother had bought me the right kind of clothes, I'd have been popular in school and my whole life would have been different. *If only* my parents hadn't broken up, I wouldn't have ended up divorced, too. *If only* I'd been a boy (or a girl), or been smarter (or prettier or a better athlete), my father would have loved me.

Some *if only*'s seem to originate in adult years. *If only* I had (or hadn't) married X, I could have had such a great life. *If only* I had (or hadn't) bought that stock, I'd be rich today. But it usually turns out that adult *if only*'s are simply extensions of *if only* habits that go back to childhood. The woman who says *if only* about her husband today probably said *if only* about her father when she was a child.

If only's are sometimes expressed as *I should have* or *I could have* or *Why didn't I?* All such phrases indicate the intention to remain unhappy until someone or something changes in the past. Sometimes that "someone" is ourselves and that "something" is our own behavior.

171

Forgiveness Begins at Home

Fifty-year-old Mark, a manager of an electronics store, was chronically depressed. His second wife, Veronique, had filed for divorce and the daughter of his first marriage, Tina, hadn't spoken to him for at least a year.

When asked how things had been when Tina was a child, Mark admitted to failing her badly. "Her mother and I shared joint custody, and Tina spent every other week with Veronique and me. Her mother was depressed and would send her for visits dressed in messy clothes, her hair too tangled to get a brush through.

"Veronique resented having someone else's child around. She was cold to Tina, for example not letting her hang posters in her room. I put up with Veronique doing this because I found I couldn't change it, and I just decided that making my marriage work was more important.

"Looking back, it all seems so obvious. I could have bought Tina a separate wardrobe to wear at my house. I could have laundered the clothes she brought, so she'd have something decent to wear at her mother's. I could have taken her to a hair salon and had her shampooed. I could have shampooed it myself and rinsed the tangles out. If only I'd helped her instead of lecturing her! If only I'd been more playful and affectionate instead of critical!"

He broke off, looking desperate, and I asked him, "What are you feeling?"

"Ashamed," he sighed. "If only I could go back and do it right."

In imagination, Mark needed to return to his early years and see when he'd made his decision to sell himself out and heap himself with shame. For the moment, however, it seemed more urgent to encourage him not to heap on even more. I urged him to credit himself for his courage in confronting such painful truths and for his willingness to change.

Acknowledging his responsibility helped Mark to overcome his depression. In time, he accepted that nothing he could do in the present would change the past, and that Tina might never forgive him. All he really could do, he decided, was to work on changing his own shame-based behavior.

I suggested that Mark start writing frequent letters to Tina, but not send them. He did this for a while, then eventually wrote one that he thought worth sending.

> Dear Tina,
>
> As you know, Veronique and I are getting divorced. This has been the occasion for me to replay our marriage in memory. And when I think of you at twelve years old asserting your right to order your room to your desire (after all, it *was* your room) and Veronique's desire to control, I am deeply sorry I did not stand up for you. I wish I could play it over differently.
>
> Tina, there is so much I could tell you and I can only hope that someday you will provide the opportunity. I've heard you say, "Don't call me, Dad." I respect your request and admire your clarity. It would be dumb to walk through some trivial ritual conversation when we are both hurting.
>
> Since I expect to have a long life, I hope the time will come when you will allow me to make peace with you. Tina, I'm learning a lot these days. How lucky I am that one of my children is you, my only daughter. Perhaps down the road, we can get to know each other in new ways.
>
> Please take good care of yourself. I hope someday to tell you how precious you are to me and to list the many ways I respect you and all you have done to be as strong as you are. I love you, Tina.
>
> Dad

Writing this letter left Mark relatively peaceful. So far, Tina has not responded, but Mark hopes the letter lays the groundwork for a future bridge. If that should happen, Mark will be ready. If not, at least he will no longer be repressing and depressing huge parts

173

of himself. He cannot redeem the past, but he can have a better future.

The Power of the Letter

Letters have enormous power. Irreparable harm is often done to relationships by sending the kind of letters that should never be sent. Letters full of rage, pain, accusation, pleading, or suffering put the receiver on the defensive and invite counterattacks that may escalate out of control. Yet great healing is often achieved by writing exactly the same sort of letters, filling them with every last bit of your rage, and then *not* sending them.

Our society is not comfortable with the so called "negative" emotions. Instead, it stigmatizes them with ugly names. Complaints of pain are labeled as "self-pity." Rage is called "being out of control." Mourners are told not to cry. Obsessions and repetition compulsions feed on this sort of repression. Lately, grief therapy has been devised for the bereaved who have trouble getting over their losses. It consists of little more than encouraging a survivor to devote several days exclusively to looking at old pictures, talking of the loved one, and weeping till the tears run out. In many cases, clients emerge from the experience able to enjoy life for the first time in years.

Oppressive anger can be relieved in much the same way. The more totally we give ourselves to any intense emotion, the more quickly it may pass, leaving us open to other feelings. The trouble is that few of us know how to express anger without harming or provoking others. The unsent letter is an ideal method. The following is an excerpt from an unsent letter from a daughter to her father:

> I remember when you and my mother broke up. It was the most miserable time of my life. You came over one day and found me crying. All you could say was, "Are you having your period?" God, what a stupid, sick bastard you are. I would have been better off in an institution, in an orphanage, given

174

up for adoption, anything! I would not have missed you. NOT AT ALL!!!!

You said I ruined your life. How could you be so pathetic? *YOU ruined your own life.* You never did anything worthwhile. You were a screwup. You are a failure as a husband, as a father, as a businessman. You've alienated almost everyone in your life!

This letter goes on for twenty handwritten pages. It might take two such letters or ten or a hundred to bring the writer's anger entirely into the open air and burn it off. But sooner or later the fuel is bound to run out. No one can weep or rage forever. Sooner or later, we get tired or bored and start thinking of other things.

Deplete your store of tears or anger by writing letters. Once you calm down, in fact, you'll find a whole store of other feelings waiting to be expressed, possibly including tenderness and nostalgia. Don't be bothered if you get too "soft." You needn't show anyone your unsent letters.

Impossible Partners

The purpose of the unsent letters is to ventilate your old feelings, to acquaint you with your old decisions, and to complete the past. It's like razing an old building and clearing the ground. The purpose of the redecision process is to decide what to build instead, to establish a new foundation. If, ultimately, you find that reconciliation is possible, that's wonderful. But sometimes the result may be a decision *not* to reconcile. There are some fathers and daughters who are better off without each other.

There would be no point for a father to attempt a relationship with the equivalents of King Lear's older daughters. Regan and Goneril feel only contempt for their father and don't care what becomes of him once they get their hands on his property.

Some fathers also are too toxic to approach. One young mother who had been sexually abused by her father sentimentally reconciled with him in adulthood, only to discover later on that he used the opportunity to molest her own small daughter.

Particularly dangerous are fathers whose professed love for a child is wielded as a weapon against the child's mother. The poet, Lord Byron, was that kind. "Mad, bad, and dangerous to know," his lover, Caroline Lamb, once called him. His daughters might have said the same.

As great a celebrity in his own day as Elvis Presley was in his, Byron wrote much scathing satire aimed at intellectual women, especially those with scientific interests:

> 'Tis pity learned virgins ever wed
>> With persons of no sort of education
> Or gentlemen who, though well born and bred,
>> Grow tired of scientific conversation;
> I don't choose to say much upon this head,
>> I'm a plain man, and in a single station,
> But—Oh! ye lords of ladies intellectual,
> Inform us truly, have they not hen-peck'd you all?

The main target of these attacks was Byron's divorced wife, a mathematician in a day when virtually no women studied mathematics. A month or two after their daughter, Ada, was born, Byron left England forever amid rumors (mainly true) of wife beating, bisexuality, and incest with his half sister. From a distance, he publically wooed little Ada in verse, trying to turn her against her mother:

> Ada! Sole daughter of my house and heart . . . !
> My daughter! with thy name this song begun—
> I see thee not—I hear thee not—but none
> Can be so wrapped in thee . . .
>
> To hold thee lightly on a gentle knee,
> And print on thy soft cheek a parent's kiss,

This, it should seem, was not reserved for me;
Yet this was in my nature . . .

I know that thou wilt love me; though to drain
My blood from out thy being were to be an aim
And an attainment—all would be in vain—
Still wouldst thou love me. . . .

Raised by her mother, Ada became an inventor. When the owner
of a textile factory sought an automatic weaving process, she successfully created the world's first computer language and program.
Her achievement, so remarkable for a Victorian woman, is still
honored. The compiler language, ADA, used by the U.S. federal
government, was named for her, along with many electronics products and companies, such as ADATECH.

Would Byron's little Ada have become the world's first major
female inventor if her father had been in charge of her education?
Far less likely.

Despite his proclamations in verse, Ada was not even Byron's
"sole daughter." Less than a year after her birth, another girl was
born to him by one of his discarded mistresses. The man who made
such a public fuss over Ada dumped her baby sister in an Italian
convent, where he never visited her and forbade the nuns to let her
desperate mother visit her either. She died there at the age of five.

Plainly, Byron's sentimental passion for Ada was due less to his
wish to cherish a daughter than to his vengeful feelings toward his
ex-wife and all women. An only child, Byron had lost his drunken
wastrel of a father when he was three and was raised thereafter by
a violent, possibly psychotic, mother. His anger toward her was
later expressed as destructiveness toward both his female lovers
and his female children.

Fathers like Byron, who proclaim great love while practicing
abandonment and abuse, are dangerous. We see this type today
among divorced fathers who refuse to pay support, yet vindictively
abduct their children or file nuisance suits over their custody.

Often, like Byron, they are themselves adult children of abandonment and abuse. Yet, no matter how sad the circumstances that created such a father, his daughter is usually better off without him.

When Love Means Living Under Tyranny

When she first joined group therapy, Maggie was thirty years old—a tall, attractive redhead and a graduate of Yale and of Harvard Law School. Working as an associate in a large and prestigious firm, she made an excellent salary. Her main problem in life, she said, was Gunther, the senior partner who supervised her work.

Maggie was the abused daughter who cried when she saw *La Traviata* and whose father made her eat the chocolate liqueur candies at the airport. Here is the story of how she came to recognize her father-based decisions and to change them.

"Last Friday evening, I had a seven-thirty date. I told Gunther I had to leave by seven. So what did he do? At quarter to seven, he dumped a pile of work on my desk and told me he needed it by midnight. I couldn't risk my job. I had to call off my date."

Maggie coughed and choked as she told her story. At work, she said, she "couldn't catch her breath." When she thought about her educational debts, she "just couldn't breathe." Her whole life, it seemed, was one long process of slow suffocation.

I asked whether there was anything she'd rather do than practice law. She answered that she had always wanted to be a screenwriter, but that she had chosen the law because writing was so much harder.

"Writing's harder than the law?" I questioned.

She nodded emphatically. "Oh, it is. Much harder. You do reasonably well in law school and it's practically automatic that you can get a well-paying job. But writing is a very risky business. Most screenwriters are not successful."

I asked her when "not being successful" had become an issue and she described a scene when she was about thirteen. "My

178

mother and I were with some company when my father barged into the room. He was carrying my sister's diaper, all stinking with poo. My sister is handicapped and at six she was still wearing diapers. He flung this thing across the room at my mother and said, 'This belongs to *your* child. Go take care of her!' The point is, Dad always referred to Donna as my mother's child because she was imperfect. But when I did something to boast about, when I was successful, then I was *his*—Daddy's Little Girl."

I then asked Maggie to go back to a childhood scene when she had wanted to do one thing but felt she had to do another, and to tell it in the present tense.

She answered immediately, with some bitterness. "I want to play the trumpet in the school jazz band, and the music teacher says, 'I would rather have you play the oboe. It's harder for me to get oboe players than trumpet players. Besides, we can lend you an oboe free, but you'd have to buy a trumpet.' " But the whole point for me is that I'd seen a woman trumpet player in a jazz group at Mardi Gras, and I could just see myself playing the trumpet like her and having a wonderful time. That's why I want to learn it."

"So, what do you do?"

"What my teacher wants. I take up the oboe. But I hate it, so I quit the band next year."

"Any scenes with your father around musical instruments?"

"Yes. He wanted me to learn the organ. I hated the organ, but I wanted to please him so I did it. Every day, after school, I'd have to practice, and I'd feel sick to my stomach with dread. I can still feel him poking me in the back with his fingers, to get me to sit up straight."

I handed her an inflated Indian club. "Go on," I said. "Pretend the pillow on that couch is your father. Go tell him how you feel about your organ lessons and your sister's diaper. Give him a good punch in the head if that's what you feel like doing."

Maggie took the Indian Club and approached the pillow uneasily. Apparently, she felt shy performing like this in front of a group. "Dad," she said softly, "I don't like a lot of things you did."

179

"Say it louder," I suggested.

She raised her voice slightly. "Dad, I'm very angry about that diaper. You humiliated Mother and me. And that organ. I'm still angry at the way you forced it on me."

"Louder," I said.

Suddenly she let loose with a blow to the pillow. "Dad, I'm telling you once and for all! I don't want your organ!"

The whole room burst into laughter. When things were quiet again, Maggie told him, more calmly, "Daddy, I'm not going to do what you want anymore, just to get your approval. From now on, I'm doing what I want."

Maggie was now ready to rewrite the two crucial decisions of her childhood. Going back to early scenes, she told her father that from now on she was going to pursue the career that she wanted, whether he approved or not. She also told herself that not all men were her father and she could be safe with some of them. If a man started bullying, she could tell him off and go away. She didn't have to work for men like Gunther. There were other jobs.

Like Mayan in *The Lost Father*, Maggie had accepted that her father was "just a man," one flawed human being among a billion others. Like Mayan, she found that she could still make room for him in her life, but at the periphery, not at the center.

Maggie's redecision did not transform her life overnight. She had new directions to choose, new habits to build. But it was the crucial change that made the other changes possible. Maggie had been the victim daughter of an abusive father. Typically, she had decided early that she was too unimportant to do what she wanted and had let the demands of others control her. Through her redecisions, she took control of her own life.

Practicing Redecision

Although redecision is usually done with an experienced therapist, individuals can practice it on their own. Some may prefer doing it entirely in their heads or in writing, but most will benefit from the dramatic immediacy of speaking aloud and using the two-chair method, as demonstrated in our case histories. What's most important is to take the steps in order:

Describe how you'd like to change your relationship with your father or daughter (or any other).

Choose a recent example of your acting in the way that you want to change, either with that other or someone else.

Describe that event as if it were happening here and now.

Describe how you feel reliving the event.

Describe the feelings that you are left with when it's over.

Look back in your imagination to the earliest similar event that you can remember and say when, where, and what it was. Make sure it's an event that involved the other.

Describe that early event as if it were happening here and now.

Go back over the two scenes and notice
    a) which feelings are similar
    b) which beliefs are similar
    c) which choices of response are similar.

Say more about these similarities.

Now, go back to the scene from your past and speak for the other person, sitting in her or his chair. Tell the whole event from the other's point of view.

Return to your own chair and reply. What do you say in response to the other's viewpoint?

You are still in the past. What was your decision?

Would you be willing to stick with this decision for
    ——ten years? ——five years? ——two years?
    ——one year? ——one month? ——a lifetime?

181

What would you be willing to do instead?

Say so to the other party.

Sit in the other's chair and reply to you. What would the other think of your redecision?

Return to your own chair. How would you reply? Notice if your reply suggests that you can't change until the other does.

If so, rephrase your response to indicate that you're going to change whether the other changes or not.

Repeat your intention to change, experimenting with the language, until you find the phrasing that expresses what you mean most clearly and forcefully.

What was your original decision?

What is your redecision?

How do you feel now?

Redecisions for Fathers and Daughters

Although every father and daughter pair is unique, there are certain typical decisions and redecisions that drive the six dances described in chapters 2 through 7. Characteristically, these "decisions" are made early, outside of consciousness, and tend to be harmful; whereas the later "redecisions" are conscious, deliberate choices, intended to change life for the better.

Lost Father/ Yearning Daughter
His decision: Closeness and vulnerability are dangerous.
Her decision: I'm not lovable. I'd better choose unavailable men who will never get to know me.
His redecision: It's all right to get close to people, to love my daughter, to be playful sometimes.

182

Her redecision: I'm lovable even if my father didn't love me. I can choose to love men who are available.

Abusive Father/Victim Daughter

His decision: It's a dangerous world. I must control people by frightening and hurting them.

Her decision: I'm not important. My well-being is insignificant.

His redecision: I will stop trying to control people by harming them, even if I have to give up alcohol or drugs to do it.

Her redecision: I'm important, and I am going to protect, care for, and nurture myself.

Pampering Father/Spoiled Daughter

His decision: I'm not lovable, so I have to buy love.

Her decision: I can't survive without some man to support and coddle me.

His redecision: I can be loved for myself. I don't have to make someone dependent on me to get love.

Her redecision: I can learn to take care of myself and love men for what they are, not for what they give.

Pygmalion Father/Companion Daughter

His decision: I will use my daughter to create something wonderful.

Her decision: I owe my power and worth to my father.

His redecision: I can let go of my daughter and create something wonderful on my own.

Her redecision: I can let go of my father and discover my own worth and power.

Ruined Father/Rescuing Daughter

His decision: If I act helpless, I'll get my mother back.

Her decision: I'm not important or lovable. I have to buy acceptance by sacrificing myself and rescuing others.

His redecision: I'm not helpless and my daughter is not my mother. If I truly need care, others can also provide it.

Her redecision: I'm as lovable and important as anyone else. I don't have to sacrifice to be acceptable.

Anguished Father/Angry Daughter

His decision: I'm a helpless victim of female anger.

Her decision: My anger is my only defense against abuse and exploitation.

His redecision: I don't need to be a victim. I have other choices beside throwing myself on my daughter's mercy.

Her redecision: I can find other ways to assert myself besides anger. I can be healthy even if my father is sick.

Another View of the Repetition Compulsion

When we look at these suggested redecisions, several points stand out.

First, the issues that they represent for each type of father and daughter are not confined to the father-daughter relationship. Abusive fathers tend to be abusive with many people, not just daughters. Angry daughters tend to go through life being angry at lovers, children, and even strangers. In cases where this rule seems not to hold, it usually turns out that the person has merely switched roles in the drama triangle. A victim daughter may become a persecuting mother, for example, treating her child the way she was treated, or she may be involved in trying to rescue. But whether as victim, persecutor, or rescuer, she remains entangled in abusive relationships.

The second point is that father-daughter issues tend to generate vicious circles. A remote father creates powerful yearnings for closeness in his daughter. But because he fears closeness, the more she shows her neediness, the more he may back away. That's why we call these interrelationships dances. The partners are caught in a kind of lockstep, one moving backward when the other moves forward, and the reverse.

184

Family therapist Harville Hendrix, Ph.D., author of *Getting the Love You Want* and *Keeping the Love You Find,* describes the complementary problems of lovers.[7] In most cases, he observes, *people end up with exactly the partners most likely to frustrate and annoy them.* For example, cool, remote men and excitable, demonstrative women often marry each other. Likewise, sociable types choose loners, worriers wed the reckless, and peace-loving souls find themselves with partners who love to fight.

In a society where people select their own mates, this tendency cannot be coincidental. People actually choose these "incompatible" partners! But why? Because they want to be miserable? On the contrary, says Hendrix.

Hendrix argues that we choose partners with whom we can pick up where we left off with our parents. Such partners will have many of our parents' traits, both those we loved and those we hated. At the same time, we pick partners who embody the undeveloped parts of ourselves, being strong where we are weak or weak where we are strong.

Hendrix's theory helps to explain why opposites first attract and then repel each other. For example, Janet, who is vivacious and warm, is attracted to Jim, who is calm and controlled, because Janet's father was calm and controlled and also because calm and control are what she lacks in herself. After a couple of years, however, Janet comes to see Jim's calm as unresponsiveness. Jim, meanwhile, is at first enchanted by Janet's warmth and vivacity, which he lacks and therefore craves, and which he unconsciously associates with his mother. But since Jim has a deep-rooted pattern of squelching emotion and rejecting his mother, it isn't long before he starts finding fault with Janet.

Partners like Jim and Janet, says Hendrix, are seeking what they need to become whole. What they look for in others is what they have rejected in themselves. And what they reject in themselves is what the experience of their childhood taught them to reject, often because it conflicted with their parental programming.

This is a very exciting idea. As Hendrix sees it, friction arises

185

between couples at the very points where both are most in need of change. Thus, Jim accuses Janet of being out of control and Janet accuses Jim of being overcontrolled; and both are right. The problem is that they're far too busy blaming each other and defending themselves to see how right the partner is. If Jim and Janet only realized that their original attraction was based on the match of their problems, they could become partners in mutual growth instead of harm. Much of this theorizing can apply to fathers and daughters, too.

Hendrix also helps us to understand the potential value of the repetition compulsion. It's not there to torment or destroy us but to keep confronting us with our unresolved issues from childhood until we do something about them. He also helps us to understand why we can't escape the past by running away from it, and why working out our relationships not only restores the other person to us but also restores us to ourselves. As the theologian Lewis Smedes wrote:

> Love will not let you lock yourself into the prison cell of your bitter memories. It will not permit you the demeaning misery of wallowing in yesterday's pain. Your love for yourself will generate enough energy, finally, to say, "I have had enough; I am not going to put myself down by letting somebody's low blow keep hurting me forever."

10

GETTING CLOSER

◆

If you cannot get rid of the
family skeleton, make it dance.

—George Bernard Shaw

If Harville Hendrix is right and there is more potential for growth
in salvaging relationships than in dumping them, the question
remains how the salvaging is to be done. Just as our society lacks
constructive models for expressing negative emotions, it also lacks
sufficient models for resolving conflicts. People who have difficulty
with family members are often advised to get out of the relationship and are labeled "codependents" if they don't. After all, if
things have always been bad and they show no sign of getting
better, staying in can truly be a torment.

Malcolm and Lucinda

Malcolm, who is seventy-six, is the wealthy, retired father of
thirty-seven-year-old Lucinda, the youngest of his three children
and the only girl. Lucinda, a twice-divorced and childless romance
writer, collects no alimony and earns under twenty thousand dollars a year. She is able to maintain a comfortable life-style only by
taking a monthly allowance from her father.

Lucinda sees the allowance as a kind of advance on her inheritance and as owed to her. Malcolm sees himself as supporting a grown but childish woman, which gives him the right to show his contempt and offer endless advice. Malcolm feels disappointed in Lucinda, and Lucinda feels resentful toward Malcolm—exactly the feelings in which they have been stewing for as long as they can remember.

Malcolm and Lucinda live fifteen hundred miles apart but quarrel as intensely as if they were under the same roof. Month after month, Malcolm "forgets" to send the money, and Lucinda has to start phoning him with "reminders," sometimes grimly pleading, sometimes furiously demanding. Malcolm eventually does send the check, but only after humiliating Lucinda with reminders of her dependency. As soon as one check arrives, Lucinda starts worrying about the next. Lord Byron described the English winter as "ending in July, to recommence in August." Malcolm and Lucinda's monthly money game no sooner ends than it begins again.

Malcolm and Lucinda's game has been going on since Lucinda was a little girl. Malcolm has always used money to control Lucinda, and Lucinda has always resented it. She is still waiting for him to become generous; he is still waiting for her to become grateful.

In psychological terms, a "game" is a transaction between two people which allows both of them to wind up feeling bad. To an uninvolved observer, Malcolm and Lucinda's behavior is clearly a game and looks easy enough to stop. All it would take is for Malcolm to send the monthly checks on time or for Lucinda either to earn more money or to learn to live on her present earnings. But neither seems inclined to make such a change. The game fits their repetition compulsions too well.

But what if, one day, Malcolm should say to Lucinda, "Is what I'm sending enough, darling? Couldn't you use some more?" or if Lucinda should announce, "I won't be needing the allowance from now on," or even "I'm so grateful to you, Dad. Your support is allowing me to do the work I love." Would the other even hear?

Would the message be dismissed as "too late"? Or is it possible that the whole relationship would open up?

Blind-Alley Relationships

Malcolm and Lucinda are in a blind-alley relationship. Most blind-alley relationships consist of three phases:

Pretense: politeness masking negative feelings
Chaos: negative feelings destructively expressed
Avoidance: shunning each other.

Some fathers and daughters concentrate on one phase—pretending, or fighting, or avoiding each other most of the time. Others shuttle between two phases, and still others get into a cycle that includes all three.

Malcolm and Lucinda are an interesting case in that they keep all three phases going at once. Malcolm pretends to be a loving, generous father by giving Lucinda an allowance, while Lucinda pretends to be a cooperative daughter in order to get it. Malcolm expresses his hostility by sending the money late, while Lucinda shows hers by nagging and complaining. Both maintain avoidance by living far apart and seldom meeting. Also, Lucinda tells her father almost nothing that goes on in her life.

Libby, Ed, and Pretense

Repeatedly cycling through the stages is a more common approach.

Libby is thirty-three, a divorced office manager with a nine-year-old son. She makes a concerted effort to avoid disputes with Ed, her widowed father, who has always been something of a bully. Ordinarily, whether she agrees with him or not, she murmurs something that sounds like agreement. She tells herself that he's a

189

stubborn old coot and that nothing she could say would change him, so why bother?

Inevitably, though, the time comes when Libby gets fed up and a quarrel ensues. It happened, for example, when her sister married a man named Rick, whom Ed detested. Every time Ed and Libby got together, Ed would criticize Rick. Because she liked Rick, Libby found the situation intolerable.

She could imagine herself calmly telling her father how she felt. "Look, Dad, I know what you think of Rick, but I happen to like him. So, would you please not criticize him to me anymore?"

Her dream was that Ed would reply, "Hell, Libby, why didn't you say so? Look, if that's how you feel, we won't talk about him." Her experience told her that he'd probably bellow, "Who the hell are you to dictate what I can say and can't say? The guy's a jerk and I'll say it every hour on the hour if I feel like it."

Afraid of a confrontation, Libby kept silent for many months, clinging to pretense out of a fear of chaos.

Libby, Ed, and Chaos

Libby feared her father's temper. Even more, she feared her own. Like many dominated people, she knew she had a powerful store of anger inside and was afraid of what would happen if she tapped into it. In books, plays, and movies, chaos often leads to a resolution. People tell each other off; truth is revealed; the good guy gives the bad guy his just punch in the nose; the audience goes away feeling satisfied. In real life, it seldom works that way, and the momentary exhilaration and relief of the explosion are followed by a whole new set of problems. Knowing this, Libby maintained her pretense of being at peace.

Then Ed said something particularly provocative, and she exploded. Forgetting her careful speech, she let her rage spew out. "Will you kindly shut up about Rick!" she screamed. "I'm sick of the way you put him down. Rick is ten times the man you'll ever be. He's a sweet, loving guy, and you're a cruel, critical bastard." She followed this up with examples of Ed's ill behavior, examples that she had been hoarding ever since the last explosion.

Ed exploded in return. He shouted her down, calling her a damned fool for not seeing through Rick and an ungrateful bitch for yelling at him that way. He added that it was no wonder her husband had left her. All his lifelong dissatisfactions with her character poured out.

Libby, Ed, and Avoidance

After unloading her resentments, and being wounded by Ed's retorts, Libby stormed out of his house—face flushed, heart pounding, shouting over her shoulder that she never wanted to see him again. Ed phoned Libby's son, to tell him that "your mom won't allow your grampa in her house any more." The boy, who was deeply attached to his grandfather, became angry with Libby, who told herself that she and the boy would both be better off without that evil old man.

Libby, Ed, and Renewing the Cycle

After some weeks, when the rage began to cool, different feelings came to the fore. Libby saw that her son missed his grandfather and blamed her for the separation. In a way, she missed her father, too. Finally, she phoned him, inviting him to Sunday dinner. He had missed her, too, and came gladly. A period of wary pretense followed, during which both parties avoided sensitive subjects. Then Ed began to make snide comments again, which Libby overlooked in order to avoid another fight. As his boldness increased, so did her suppressed anger, and another storm became inevitable.

In the Loop

To the observer, it's clear that Libby and Ed are in a loop they can't get out of. When they're in pretense, things are quiet but resentments are accumulating. When they're in chaos, they get emotional release but at the price of fresh wounds. When they're in avoidance, they feel liberated, yet bitterness and yearning are both sure to follow.

Like Malcolm and Lucinda, they're playing a game, hurting themselves compulsively, without conscious awareness. It doesn't seem it would take much to stop. All Ed has to do is quit making provocative remarks. All Libby has to do is to leave the room, change the subject, or stop taking the bait. But, as anyone knows who's ever been in such a relationship, changing lifelong patterns of behavior is exceedingly difficult to do.

Intimacy

Why do people play these dreadful games? Why do we get caught in the loop of pretense, chaos, and avoidance? One theory is that such behaviors are ways to avoid intimacy—that is, emotional closeness based on openness and honesty.

There are many reasons to avoid that much closeness—above all, the fear of rejection and the fear of betrayal. As we have seen, some men associate women with treachery, and some women, of course, fear their fathers. With distrust on both sides, there's plenty of reason to back off. Yet intimacy is the only alternative to the cycle of *pretense, chaos,* and *avoidance.*

M. Scott Peck, M.D., is a psychiatrist and author of *The Different Drum: Community Making and Peace,* which describes how "communities" are built.[1] According to Peck, when people get together to form a purposeful organization, such as a political committee or a professional organization, they first meet in a condition of false congeniality he calls *pseudocommunity.* In *pseudocommunity,* everyone emphasizes similarities and minimizes differences. It's not long, however, before differences surface and the group goes into a stage that Peck calls *chaos,* in which individuals and factions quarrel without resolving anything. If the organization is to survive, says Peck, the participants must achieve *emptiness;* they must calm down and deliberately set aside their prejudices, their ideologies, and their need to convert, fix, and control. Only then can the differing factions unite into a true *community*, a cooperative enterprise capable of solving the problems that it was formed to solve.

Peck argues that *chaos* is an advance over *pseudocommunity*, because in *chaos* the problems are revealed rather than denied. But *chaos* is only useful as a transition, a step on the way to *community*.

A very similar process goes on between individuals. When people first meet, they establish what we have called *pretense*, emphasizing similarities and suppressing differences. If the relationship is to deepen, their differences must surface, eventually leading to episodes of *chaos*. At that point, the parties may go in one of three directions: they may decide the relationship is too much trouble and withdraw into *avoidance;* they may try to cover up their differences and reestablish *pretense;* or they may decide the relationship is worth making the effort to achieve *intimacy.*

If the parties fear closeness, or don't know how to achieve it, they will get into a *pretense-chaos-avoidance* loop. This is exactly the condition in which so many fathers and daughters are trapped.

What Peck says about groups is reminiscent of what Harville Hendrix says about intimate partners. Problems emerge between people at the same points where they emerge within them. Malcolm, who uses money as a weapon against his daughter Lucinda, has probably used money against many people. Libby, who puts up with her father until she explodes, probably behaves the same way toward every bully she meets.

Divesting

How do we resolve father-daughter conflicts that have gone on for years, even decades? Peck says that there is only one way—through a conscious and purposeful "emptying out" of the attitudes that underlie the conflicts. We call this process *divesting.*

When you invest in something, you buy into it. When you divest, you get rid of your bad buys. When it comes to fathers and daughters, the main goal of divesting is to get rid of habitual, outmoded, self-fulfilling concepts about what the other person is like and what the terms of the relationship have to be. Divesting is closely related to redecision.

Three ideas in particular keep father-daughter conflicts going and therefore need to be divested:

- People don't change. If our relationship didn't work in the past, it won't work in the future either.
- What my father or daughter does reflects on my own worth.
- I am an innocent victim in the relationship, but my father or daughter is a free agent.

People Don't Change

People do change, and relationships can change with them.

People change with circumstances. Alcoholics who join AA may be transformed. Finding a supportive mate, having a child, going back to school, or switching careers may turn a malcontent into a cheerful person. A religious conversion, an enlightening book, or a close encounter with death may set a life on an entirely new course.

People change with time. Fathers often "mellow" with age. A man of thirty may be too busy with his goals to notice his children; at sixty, his priorities may be very different. The father of novelist Pearl Buck was aggressively domineering through much of his life; at eighty, he was her favorite companion.

Children grow up. The father who can't relate to his thirteen-year-old may find her fascinating when she's thirty. In the film *A League of Their Own*, one of the ball players has an appalling brat of a son; in the epilogue, fifty years later, he shows up as a charming middle-aged man. The father who makes up his mind early about his children's character may miss ever getting to know them.

If one party changes in this way and the other refuses to acknowledge it, the barrier is probably the "too late" syndrome. "It's too

194

late for Dad to love me now, when I'm thirty. He should have done it when I was thirteen." "Don't tell me Mary's settled down. She's still that same spiteful brat who needed an abortion at fifteen." In dealing with people who have hurt us, caution should always be used, of course. No former molester, however repentant, should be left alone with a child. No supposedly reformed thief should have access to the family safe, and no rumormonger to the family secrets. But for the father or daughter too furious about the past even to admit to the possibility of change, divesting would mean getting out of the time warp and into the here and now.

What My Father or Daughter Does Reflects on My Own Worth

In 1989, in St. Louis, a sixteen-year-old high-school student named Tina Issa was murdered by her immigrant parents, who justified their act by calling it an "Honor Death." According to a report on *60 Minutes,* Tina had been killed because she defied her father's order to give up her boyfriend and her job at McDonald's. Her parents had immigrated from a country where girls are not allowed to date, earn spending money, or argue with their fathers. As they saw it, Tina's Americanized behavior was a disgrace that could be wiped out only by her death.

At one time or another, most of us have been embarrassed by a family member. Feeling ashamed of one's parents is almost a teenage American rite of passage. A daughter may blush at her father's appearance, profession, accent, or any other trait that differs from the social ideal. A father may feel ashamed of a daughter who is plain, unpopular, a "bimbo," or a "whore."

Treating people who love us as if they were stains on our clothing can cause devastating pain. Jed, a lawyer with two daughters, strongly favored one of them. One day he was lunching with the other, whose name was Eileen. An associate from his office stopped by their table, and the father introduced Eileen as his daughter. "Oh," said the associate, "you're visiting from Paris, are you?"

"No, my sister lives in Paris," Eileen told him. "I live right here in Boston." "Oh, I didn't know Jed had a daughter here in Boston," the associate said, unthinkingly telling Eileen just how low she stood in her father's estimation.

Those who regard family members as objects of shame seldom really see them. Tina Issa was at the top of her high-school class. Eileen was a talented woman who became a university professor. Children can also fail to see their parents' true worth. Many children of immigrants haven't the least idea of the heroic courage required to leave one's native land, learn a new language, and adapt to a new culture.

Being ashamed of a family member is rooted in prejudice. Intimacy is impossible with a person we are prejudiced against, or who is prejudiced against us.

I Am an Innocent Victim; Others Are Free Agents

Even adult children can feel like their parents' innocent victims. The sense of helpless innocence began in childhood, when we were so small and they were so big. Many adolescents still see their parents as godlike, holding them personally responsible for the condition of the planet, for wars and social injustice. Yet the parents of our childhood were no more powerful than we are now, and as they grow older, we steadily become more powerful than they. Recognizing this one plain truth can be a tremendous help to a daughter in divesting herself of old attitudes.

Parents may also grant their children imaginary powers. Some expect them to justify the parents' existence through spectacular beauty, genius, or accomplishments. If the child fails to live up to such demands, the parent may blame the child and see himself as her victim.

Parental ideologies can ruin a relationship at any stage. When Catherine was thirty-two years old, a tenured professor, married to a collegiate dean, and the mother of three, her father discovered that she had become slack in her church attendance. "I always knew you'd turn out no good," he raged. "Worthless! You don't even love your God." A daughter's ideology can do the same harm. The famous "generation gap" of the sixties consisted mainly of young people repudiating their parents over ideological differences. A slogan like "Never trust anyone over thirty" leaves little room for parent-child reconciliation.

The First Steps Toward Intimacy

Let's say you agree on the necessity of breaking the cycle of *pretense, chaos,* and *avoidance.* Let's say you've begun the job of divesting yourself of detrimental ideas. What next? How do you behave in your father's or daughter's company? How do you begin the approach?

Fortunately, there are a number of steps you can take which are quite low risk and not difficult.

Introducing a New Topic—Lucinda, Malcolm, and Der Rosenkavalier

Lucinda and Malcolm probably sound like a boring pair, with their perpetual bickering over her allowance. Yet, on their own, they are intelligent, interesting people. The problem is, they don't show each other their positive qualities or encourage them in each other.

Imagine Lucinda phoning her father one day. Ordinarily, she would begin by saying with a sigh, "Dad, it's the eighth of the month and the check's still not here." Today, instead, she asks excitedly, "Dad, do you remember when I was about fifteen and you took me to the Met to see *Der Rosenkavalier?* Well, I've just started writing a new historical romance set in Vienna, and it brought back that memory so vividly that I rented the video. Can you remember who was in it? It was Kiri Te Kanawa on the video, but that would have been before her time."

Perhaps all this sounds comical, unthinkable, impossible. *My*

197

God! You can't talk to your father as if he were a real person! You can't discuss things you're really interested in! But why not?

Good relationships are based on pleasure, not pain. You and your friends don't spend all your time together wrestling with or attempting to suppress painful issues. You don't glare at one another or suffer torments of guilt over events of years ago. You get together to enjoy yourselves. So, if your relationship with your father or daughter is poor, it's probably because you never learned how to enjoy each other, or you've forgotten how, or you let unpleasant memories and habits stand in the way.

People whose relationships are strained will not want to discuss intensely personal topics. *Der Rosenkavalier* is not personal, although it touches upon a shared experience. Approaching someone through a common interest is one of the surest yet safest ways to begin, because it creates warmth without generating heat. Even if Malcolm should grumpily reply that he doesn't remember, Lucinda has lost nothing.

Lightening Up

As a teen, Jayne had resented her overprotective, widowed father. Now a fun-loving young woman in her twenties, she had come to hate how defensive she felt when he and his new wife were around. One evening, her father phoned to announce that they would be passing through town the following week. Hanging up, Jayne decided she couldn't stand another meeting like the last.

Within seconds of greeting her father and his wife, she presented them with a welcoming gift: a Rube Goldberg–style contraption whose purpose they were to guess. Her stepmother solved the problem, then retaliated by throwing riddles at Jayne. The three of them had an uproarious time throughout the visit and parted feeling that their problems were settled, even though not a word had been said about them.

Relations between fathers and daughters are heavy with the weight of the past. Any lightening up will help. It's not mandatory to resolve every issue, to decide who was wrong and who was right about some past event, or even to make apologies and receive them, in order to get out of the *pretense-chaos-avoidance* loop. Sometimes all it takes is to behave as if the relationship were already the way that you wish it could be.

Reenvisioning the Other

Another way to break the cycle is to reenvision your parents, to see them clearly in another time and place.

If your family has old home movies, convert them to videotape. Put on your favorite background music, something relaxing and tender and dreamy. Sit back and watch the tape to the accompaniment of the music.

If you're a daughter, watch your parents' wedding or honeymoon, or their pride in you when you were small. If you're a father, remember how sweet, how vulnerable, how loving your daughter was as a little girl. If they have changed for the worse since then, let yourself feel the sadness of it, the waste of an opportunity for happiness.

Imagine your father or daughter there on the screen as someone you don't know—someone else's relative, or a character in a drama on TV. Let it sink in that the person you blame for your pain is only a person—a human being, not a fallen idol—someone who has also been hurt by life.

If old home movies or videotapes are not available, then turn on the soothing music and look through old family picture albums. Look for scenes in which you and your father or daughter were holding each other. Appreciate the love that was once between you.

Dumping Father and Daughter Subpersonalities

Early on, fathers and daughters develop characteristic behaviors that are reserved just for each other. These behaviors grow into

199

permanent subpersonalities. Sometimes the difference between a father's "parent" subpersonality and his ordinary self can be stunning. In *The Godfather,* Vito Corleone appears to the world as a ruthless killer, yet he's an idol to his children. Singer Bing Crosby was famed for his easygoing warmth and charm, yet he was harsh and punitive with the sons of his first marriage. Daughters who can't keep out of humiliating fights with their parents may be charming to their friends and poised professionals at work. Fathers who are tactless and impatient with their daughters may be brilliantly skilled at handling people in the outside world.

An important way of breaking through father-daughter barriers is to learn to recognize your father or daughter subpersonality, and then to stop using it when it doesn't lead to the results you want. Another way is to stop believing that your father's or daughter's subpersonality is the entire person. Acknowledge that the stupefying "dad" or "kid" you've been dealing with all these years is not the real, whole person, any more than the pathetic being you are in that person's presence is the real, whole you.

By dumping your unloving subpersonality, you can model the kind of behavior you wish to evoke. By showing the other more of yourself, you make it safer for the other to do the same.

Put Your Childhood into Perspective

Painful as some of your memories may be, perhaps there were beneficial aspects to your childhood that you haven't considered.

In 1962, developmental psychologists Victor Goertzel and Mildred G. Goertzel published *Cradles of Eminence,* a study of the early years of the most famous and accomplished people of the twentieth century, excluding royalty.[2] Altogether, four hundred and eighteen people met their criteria, which included being listed in standard reference books and being the subject of multiple full-length biographies.

Here is what the Goertzels found:

"Normal" childhoods were rare. Only 58 out of their 418 subjects had grown up under anything like supposedly ideal circumstances—in homes where there were two parents, financial security, good health, and family harmony. The rest came from families characterized by poverty, quarrels, divorce, separation, mental problems, or alcoholism. In many cases, the parents were domineering, and there were often quarrels over the children's choices of careers or friends.

In a quarter of the cases, the children had personal problems as well: they were sickly or fat or unpopular with other children or were failures in school or handicapped in some way. Some had vision or hearing difficulties or speech defects.

What characterized them was a tendency to hypercompensate for their weaknesses. Many who were frail and sickly as children became remarkably robust adults. Many who were poor students became outstanding scholars. Many who had suffered under poverty became rich. Many who were shy became great speakers or performers. Growing up in unstable households made them strong, not weak. They had survived so much that the fear was knocked out of them.

Redefining Survivorship

Today, we often apply the word *survivor* to anyone who has managed to stay alive. Those profiled in *Cradles of Eminence* not only survived disastrous childhoods but also learned to thrive on them.

Eleanor Roosevelt was the homely daughter of fabulously beautiful parents.[3] Her mother was so repelled by Eleanor's looks that she refused to touch her. Her father loved her but was an alcoholic, often confined in institutions. When she was five, her parents separated. Shortly thereafter, her mother and a brother died of diphtheria. Because the father was institutionalized, she was put in the care of her maternal grandmother, who was ashamed of her. Her father wrote her letters promising to take her away, but he died of drink when she was ten. For the next several years, she lived in dreams of what it would have been like to be the mistress of her father's household.

She was plain, shy, clumsy, partially deaf, terrified of the dark, unpopular with other children, and unable to master spelling, grammar, or arithmetic. She lied, stole sweets, and bit her nails.

Yet this unpromising child grew up to be the wife of a dazzlingly handsome and brilliant man, the mother of five children, arguably the greatest First Lady in American history, a successful journalist, an ambassador to the United Nations, and probably the most influential woman of her time. Like anyone else, she came up against troubles throughout her life. Her mother-in-law despised her. Her husband had affairs and was also crippled by polio while their children were still young. Yet she managed to survive these ordeals, displaying far more compassion for others than pity for herself.

Redeciding About Your Childhood

The Goertzels do not recommend abusing children to turn them into Eleanor Roosevelts. But they do conclude that severely stressful childhoods are far more common than many realize and that the challenge of early stress can make as well as break people. Perhaps some individuals are born with a special capacity to endure, but decision-making clearly plays a big part. The future famous all had the ability to find whatever was positive in their environment and to build on it.

In addition to unstable homes, financial instability, and bad school experiences, many of the future famous also had unconventional and opinionated parents who made themselves unpopular by supporting minority opinions. In the vast majority of cases, at least one parent had strong intellectual interests, an admiration for achievement, and tremendous ambitions for the child. In short, the parents tended to be stubborn nonconformists who pushed their children hard.

Many children resent such parents. The future famous, in contrast, identified with and admired them. As children, they cultivated a dream of "doing it for them"—succeeding brilliantly in the very fields where their parents had failed or achieved only minor success.[4]

In the future famous, hard times in childhood tended to breed resilience, resourcefulness, a will to succeed, and a willingness to take risks. Nowadays, it's fashionable to claim that early hardships are bound to leave us "wounded." Apparently, they may also leave us toughened and inspired. It may be that the outcome depends on the decisions we make about our hardships. If we made negative decisions then, we can make positive redecisions now. And such redecisions may open the way to profoundly different relationships with family members.

Writing Unsent Letters

In the last chapter, we suggested you write letters to your father or daughter, letters that you were not to send. The purpose then was to purge your negative feelings and to express your anger. This time, we are suggesting you write for the opposite reason: to express your positive feelings—your love, appreciation, and respect.

This letter may be harder to write. There is a grim joy in tapping into pent-up anger. There can be pain in tapping into a love that you associate with sorrow. Yearnings may come to the surface that you may not have known you had, and that you may wish you didn't have, particularly if you have abandoned the other person, or been rejected, or if the other has died while you were on bad terms.

Yet, in the end, writing these letters will reward you profoundly, getting you out of denial and restoring your capacity to feel. Write as friend to friend, adult to adult, intimate to intimate, equal to equal. Confide the history of your feelings toward the person, in the security of knowing that nothing you say can be used against you. Inquire about his or her thoughts and feelings. If there's something you don't know, ask.

If the person has a truly destructive or dangerous side, write to the part uncontaminated by the evil. Express your compassion for what your father or daughter must have suffered to have turned out so badly. Express your sorrow that she or he is locked away in prison, even if only in the prison of the self. You may want to acknowledge any role that you might have played, but don't yield to the temptation of heaping blame upon yourself.

Once you feel you have had your say, then write a response from the other person to yourself. In your imagination, let the other person's soul possess you and dictate the letter. Perhaps you might continue with an exchange of letters. There could be no exercise more healing.

The Goal

Can you imagine what your father-daughter relationship could be like if both of you stopped:

> Trying to control each other?
> Trying to force your opinions on each other?
> Blaming each other for your troubles?
> Being ashamed of each other?
> Making demands on each other?
> Hating each other for not living up to expectations?

What would be left? Two human beings who loved each other despite disappointments, who supported each other's strengths and had compassion for each other's weaknesses; two human beings who meant it when they said, "Forgive us our trespasses as we forgive those who trespass against us."

11

LOVING FATHER AND LOVING DAUGHTER

◆

The approval and affirmation of others is probably the
world's most sought-after commodity. We yearn to be right
with others at the same time that we desperately need to be
true to ourselves. When the two fit together, it's heaven.[1]

—George F. Simons, *Keeping Your Personal Journal*

There probably have always been loving fathers and daughters.
Despite the patriarchy, despite the Six Dances, there must always
have been some men who affirmed their daughters' intrinsic worth
and equality, and daughters who returned that affirmation with a
sense of fellow-feeling, rather than fear, adoration, and duty.

But such relationships must have been rare. They certainly don't
show up often in recorded history and literature. Henry the Eighth
of England went through six wives in his quest to ensure his patri-
lineage. He scarcely noticed his daughter Elizabeth, who later
became the most able monarch in the nation's history. Felix and
Fanny Mendelssohn were equally gifted brother-and-sister musical
prodigies. With his family's support, Felix became a major composer. But what of Fanny? "I no longer know how one feels when
one wants to compose a song," she wrote dejectedly. "What does
it matter anyway? Nobody takes any notice . . . and nobody dances
to my tune."[2]

205

For all the broken and disrupted families we see today, there are probably more Loving Father–Loving Daughter pairs now than ever—more fathers who encourage their daughters to achieve their potential and more daughters who see their fathers as "like subjects," rather than members of some other, more powerful species.

Even so, the emergence of such pairs has been too recent to leave much of a record. How, then, can we talk about the Loving Father–Loving Daughter partnership? Perhaps the best we can do is to imagine it, to construct a model out of what records there are and what images we've seen and what some recent fathers and daughters have been trying to create. It won't be definitive, but perhaps it can provide a point of departure for fathers with small daughters to raise and father-daughter pairs exploring their relationship together.

Loving Father–Loving Daughter: A Vision

In some ways, a loving father and daughter are like any loving pair. The partners must harmonize being right with each other with being true to themselves. Sometimes this dual goal will create conflicts and one or both will be wounded. In a truly loving relationship, the wounds will be allowed to heal rather than kept open.

In other ways, a Loving Father–Loving Daughter relationship is very different. The ultimate goal, after all, is not to intensify the relationship but to give each other something of great value, then to free each other to live separate lives. Their two separate lives will always share some common ground, like a pair of partially overlapping circles; but most of the space in both their circles will be filled with other people and other pursuits.

Loving fathers and daughters will pass through many phases. There will probably always be at least some disruptions and strains during transitional periods, such as adolescence. We must also take into account that even the most nearly perfect father-daughter relationship will take place in a very imperfect world. In most cases, the sequence will go much like this:

Mutual Adoration:

The bonding phase of the loving adult-infant relationship, in which father and child see each other as perfect, wondrous, flawless beings whose wills are in natural harmony.

Relaxation:

The phase when the initial infatuation wears off, when other interests come to the fore, when some faults are recognized, but a strong bond of affection, trust, and even mutual adoration remains.

Disillusion:

The stage in which father and child are struck by the fact that the other is anything but perfect and has a separate, often contradictory, will, and in which one or both become disappointed or even angry.

Experimentation:

A period of attempts to approach and accommodate each other's differences and separateness, to set limits, to phase out controls, and to salvage the relationship.

Healing:

The process of coming to know, accept, forgive, enjoy, and rejoice in the other as whole and separate human beings—individuals and equals, living lives that are at once intimate and appropriately distanced.

Role Reversal:

The late stage when the father's age or illness may turn the child into the caretaker.

Transcendence:

The stage of acceptance, compassion, wisdom, forgiveness, farewell, and letting go.

Mutual Adoration

A father and daughter start out as apparent unequals. He is a big, strong, knowledgeable, male adult. She is a tiny, weak, ignorant, female infant. Yet, as the poet Percy Bysshe Shelley observed, "Love makes all things equal," and in terms of the joy they have to give each other, they do begin as equals.

A welcoming father quickly learns to adore his baby daughter. In his eyes, she is perfection itself. The sensuous attractions of the baby—the satiny skin and smooth limbs and small nose and big eyes—unite with the wonder of her very existence to stir powerful nurturing impulses even in some men who never suspected they were capable of such feelings.

Journalist Bob Greene writes in his journal of his daughter's first year:

> Now, though, when I'm gone . . . I physically *ache* for missing my daughter. It never seems that any story is important enough to make me not see her for another day. I know I still go out on the road all the time—but missing her is not some vague concept in my mind. It actually hurts when I think that she's at home and I'm not with her.[3]

An infant daughter quickly learns to adore her father right back, laughing, gurgling, and kicking her legs with glee at the sight of him. He is amazed that he can give her so much pleasure, merely by existing.

As we waited for a friend to arrive at the airport, we noticed a mother coming up the ramp, carrying a baby girl. They were eagerly met by a man, apparently the child's daddy. As he approached, he raised both his hands in the air with unabashed enthusiasm, saying "So big!" As the child beamed back, so did all of us strangers standing around by the gate. The two of us smiled at each other, as if to say, "That's the way!"

A loving father helps to create his loving daughter. When Martha was little, she and her dad played peek-a-boo. Sometimes she'd climb into bed, hide under the sheets, and play "You Can't Find Me." He'd pretend to look around and not see her there. When he'd give her a bath, he'd squeeze the spouting tub toys. She would laugh with delight at the sudden squirt of water, and he would laugh with equal delight at her laughter.

Loving fathers and daughters carry on a physical and emotional dialogue that makes both parties very happy. One smiles and the other smiles back. One coos and the other coos back. Daughter cries, Father picks her up, and Daughter stops crying. As Dorothy Dinnerstein observes, the great pleasure of mutually pleasurable adult sex is its resemblance to this early parent-child mutuality. Each does what feels good and the other adores it.

There's a lot to learn from observing a baby. Watching his year-old daughter feeding herself breakfast, writer Jack Kornfield learned a lesson that might have come from a Zen master:

> Caroline, who likes to eat Cheerios for breakfast, can really teach me how to live in the moment. She can sit down with her Cheerios, and line them up or put them on top of one another or spear one with her little finger or look around . . . put it in her mouth . . . chew it . . . take it out and see what happened to it . . . then stick it in my mouth to see if I like it . . . then pull it out again and spend twenty minutes experimenting with all the properties of a Cheerio. Then she'll put it down and experiment with the spoon.[4]

What a daughter of that age wants from her father is his physical presence. An infant can't appreciate the value of a paycheck. She only knows what she can see, feel, hear, touch, smell.

What she also needs from her father is validation. The women who come into therapy unsure of their worth and numbed to their own desires are women who have not had their worth and their desires validated. A father validates his daughter's desires by cheering her on as she learns to sit, crawl, stand, walk, talk, swim, ride a bicycle, and make her first wish list for Santa Claus. He continues the process later by helping with her homework and showing up for her recitals, sports events, and class plays. Still later, he gets involved in her college plans and supports the career she wants. But it all begins with being there for her first, great, fundamental achievements as an infant human being.

The first days and months of a daughter's life are the bonding phase. Basic trust is learned then. The child will always carry in her gut the experience of how she was first greeted and treated, while the father establishes the connection that will link him forever with his child, no matter how tall she grows or how far she roams.

Relaxation

Loving parents are extremely indulgent toward babies up to the age of two or so. If an infant fusses, parents will blame it on discomfort, such as hunger or teething, or on frustration over the inability to speak. But once the child reaches two or three, she is expected to start obeying and behaving and both parties start to relax their intense concentration on each other.

This shift makes perfect sense. Around two or so, the child acquires the communication skills to express her wants, become teachable, and interact more with outsiders. These same communication skills can also make her less easy to tolerate. The writhing and howling of the ten-month-old child is ambiguous. The thirty-month-old who screams "No! I don't want to! You can't make me!" leaves little to the imagination.

It's around this time that the parent-child contest of wills evolves. The parents still need to control the child, while the child is determined to get her way. The toddler's defiance implies a doubt as to whether her parents are all that perfect, after all. The parents' growing intolerance implies a doubt as to whether the flawless babe is really so flawless. It's then that the parent's love begins to be tested. Is it an unconditional love, or one conditioned on the child's living up to expectations? The child wants to know

210

"If I take an opposite position—if I'm different from you—will I still get loved?"

Little Eleanor Roosevelt, who was plain, partially deaf, and rejected by her mother, owed much to her father's unconditional love and validation. Despite his alcoholism and early death, she clung to his memory because it confirmed that someone had valued her:

> I was a shy, solemn child, even at the age of two, and I am sure that even when I danced I never smiled. My earliest recollections are of being dressed up and allowed to come down to dance for a group of gentlemen who applauded and laughed as I pirouetted before them. Finally, my father would pick me up and hold me high in the air. He dominated my life as long as he lived, and he was the love of my life for many years after he died.[5]

The daughter of silent-screen actor John Gilbert likewise never forgot how empowered she felt by her father's attention:

> I knew that he listened carefully when I talked with him and that he answered my questions thoughtfully. He wasn't like most grown-ups who would sort of half listen just long enough to catch the gist of what you were saying and then bore you to death with advice. My father asked questions. And he touched. He would brush my hair with his fingertips while he was thinking aloud or while I was telling him what I thought. He'd put down what he was doing when I spoke to him.[6]

Broadway actress Uta Hagen attributed much of her own rich sensibility to her father's training. Looking back, she wrote him this heartfelt thanks:

> What I see and smell and feel and my capability of receiving things fully comes from you and that you opened all my senses

211

to these things so early! When I walk into a cathedral and feel a vague mysteriousness of past ages first because of a musty, wood-stove incense smell, it comes as such a *memory* (not even new experience) of what you showed me, or how you stimulated emotions toward it as a child—before I could rationalize it or make it a conscious, organic part of me.[7]

Yet, in many ways, the intensity of the relationship is already subsiding. Over time, father and daughter begin to withdraw into their separate lives. The daughter starts school and becomes preoccupied with her activities and friends. Between father and daughter, things become relaxed, almost casual, foreshadowing more profound separations to come.

The loving father never lets his relaxation slide into neglect. He can go on being there for her, even when he's away. Tony LaRussa, manager of the Oakland A's, often wears an Oakland Ballet T-shirt, in honor of his two daughters who are studying dance. It's his way of saying to the world "My girls are important and what they do is important, just as important as the Oakland A's."

Democratic candidate Bill Clinton took time off from his 1992 campaign for the presidential nomination to take his daughter, Chelsea, to a dance.[8] Even after his nomination, he always flew back home when she had a ballet recital. Although many politicians exploit their children in the media, Clinton barred reporters from her activities and refused to allow the twelve-year-old to be interviewed. Such fatherly behavior announces to the world that "My daughter is more important to me than being president."

Many fathers claim not to "know what to do with a daughter." This bewilderment comes from a falsely narrow notion of the capacities and interests of little girls. A loving daughter is usually thrilled to accompany her loving father almost anywhere. Given a chance, she might enjoy fishing or computer games as much as any boy. If she happens to have more traditionally feminine interests, the father can open his mind to exploring them.

One father we interviewed was an inventor of farm machinery

who had raised a large family in the Australian bush. When asked what activities he had shared with his children, he said:

> Mostly you treat girls and boys alike, but you're aware they're different. You might be able to get down on the ground and have a wrestle with your son, but you'd fear hurting a daughter. So you become active with her in some other way, such as playing a game or singing together, or listening to the things that happen to her, with her friends or at school.
>
> I took my boys into my workshop more. The two older girls preferred dolls, and I bought them a little hand-cranked sewing machine so they could make doll's clothes. Not that the girls kept away from the workshop though. They learned turning and made furniture and lamps and also fishing reels. Lily, my baby, grew up to be a mechanic.

Disillusion

In many families, father and daughter get along fine until she reaches puberty. Then chaos breaks out. Suddenly, Daddy's endearing daughter may disappear, replaced by a temperamentally contrary but sexually attractive female with a diminished respect for Daddy's wishes or wisdom. This change of attitude is not necessarily a sign of trouble. It's part of the separation process for adolescents to withdraw from parents and turn to peers.

But adolescents aren't always ready for as much freedom as they demand, and parents aren't always willing to give them as much as they are ready for. In her memoir, *Daddyboy,* women's studies scholar Carol Wolfe Konek remembers how it was:

> He wants to keep me under his thumb. He wants me to be a baby. He thinks anyone I like only wants "one thing." He can't keep me from going anywhere, from having friends. I won't be like they are. I want friends. I want to be desired by someone who understands love.

213

"I'm going out with Alan tonight."

"No, you're not, young lady."

"I am. I'm meeting him in town at the drugstore."

"If you were going out with Alan, he would come out here and pick you up as though you were a respectable girl. He would not pick you up in town. Since, however, you are not going out, this is a moot point. You are going to stay at home, and, since it is a weeknight, you are going to study for your classes tomorrow."

"You can't keep me in this prison."

"I can keep you here and I intend to."

"You think you can keep me from him, but you can't. He loves me. We're getting married."

"You're no such thing. You're fifteen years old."[9]

In some households, fathers and adolescent daughters quarrel endlessly. Some of the issues are preposterously trivial while others are of life-determining seriousness, yet all may be fought out with the same passion. The father reads into the daughter's hairstyle the sort of recklessness that could ruin her life or disgrace the family. The daughter sees in her father's scrutiny a domineering possessiveness that could later have him running her adult life.

Great pain underlies such quarrels. To grow up, the daughter must stop idealizing her father and learn to prefer other men instead. In the process, she may become intolerant and critical, hurting him deeply. His job during these years is to accept that she will soon go away, leaving him vulnerable to feelings of rejection and resentment. In the recent film *Father of the Bride,* the humor derives from the father's attempts to sabotage his daughter's wedding, despite her obvious happiness and the groom's impeccable credentials. The father simply doesn't want her to grow up and leave.

The intensity of this conflict has grown more brutal in recent decades. A century ago, girls went through puberty in their mid-

214

teens. Today, it usually happens between ten and twelve. When physical development precedes emotional and mental development by so many years, adolescence becomes far more difficult for child and parents both.

A recent study by social historian Joan Jacobs Brumberg of Cornell University indicates that while teenaged girls of a couple of generations ago filled their diaries with reflections on "spirituality, books, intellectual and creative activities, . . . arts and games . . . and long talks with female teachers who served as mentors," today's teenaged girls "obsess about boys and body image at the expense of more fruitful activities."[10] This attitude is associated with eating disorders, sexually transmitted diseases, and early pregnancy, as well as a tendency to value thinness above either success or even love. "At a time when all kinds of new opportunities and freedoms are open to young women," says Dr. Brumberg, this adolescent body-obsession is a "national tragedy."

To help counter this destructive trend, girls need their fathers' loving validation, and their encouragement to maintain interests in more productive goals.

The loving parent of a teen must walk a tightrope. He has to be ready to let his daughter go, yet he can't do it in a way that leaves her feeling abandoned. No one can walk such a rope without sometimes losing his balance, so even the most loving father will occasionally find himself in trouble with his daughter.

He has another tightrope to walk regarding his daughter's sexual attractiveness. Many a daughter wants her father's admiration and shows herself off to him, hoping for a compliment. If she doesn't get it, she feels invalidated and unattractive. If he's too enthusiastic, she may feel embarrassed and even shamed. If he becomes sexually excited, the result may be abuse. If, to prevent that possibility, he keeps away from her, she may feel abandoned. Meanwhile, some daughters consider it sexist to be complimented for their looks at all. So even the most loving fathers and daughters are likely to suffer some feelings of resentment during these difficult years.

Experimentation

Once the daughter leaves home, life can never again be the same for the father and daughter. Instead of seeing each other in the natural course of the day, they have to plan to get together. Many fathers lose touch with their daughters during this phase. The mother writes the letters and sends the presents and talks on the phone and the father slips into the background. It's not that he doesn't care about his daughter. He simply doesn't know what to say.

Because of the tensions of the daughter's adolescence, even the most loving father and daughter often part under stress. What they need is a new basis for the relationship.

Daughters and fathers are dynamic beings. A man may become a parent at twenty-five. Twenty-five years later, his daughter may be a parent, too. During those twenty-five years, she will have moved from infancy to adulthood, gone through an education, initiated her work life and her love life, and experienced enough joys and sorrows to fill a dozen novels. He will have moved from youth to middle age and faced such trials as illness, the death of parents, war, unemployment, bankruptcy, or loss of faith, or have known soul-stretching triumphs such as career success or a deeply satisfying relationship or a religious conversion or the devotion to a cause.

They have so much to share. The problem is making it accessible to each other.

Blazin, a San Francisco artist, never felt she had much in common with her father, a retired army officer. But when she shifted from ceramics to sculpture, she discovered that he was exactly the person to teach her carpentry, welding, and similar skills. Now, when he visits her, they spend happy hours together in her studio, and when she visits him, they can't stay out of his workshop. He buys her tools for Christmas and her birthday, and she calls him long distance several times a month to brainstorm about how to overcome technical problems in her art.

There are many people in San Francisco who could give Blazin technical advice, but she takes a special joy in getting it from her father. The love has always been there. What has been lacking is the vehicle for expressing it. In their present closeness, it doesn't matter that they live two thousand miles apart. Her father is always in her studio in spirit, an active contributor to every piece of art she makes.

The experimental phase opens up new ways of knowing each other, new ways of sharing in each other's lives, no matter how many miles or years separate you. But the first requirement is to know what kind of a relationship you want.

Invitations—A Visualization

Imagine that your life is a cottage, set in a large country garden, prettily but securely fenced around, with a path leading from the house to the gate. There is a private path that leads to the house from there. If you were to invite your loving father or daughter to spend an evening with you, perhaps a birthday, which would you arrange?

- Meeting at the gate, then going to some public place, like a restaurant, movie, or sports event?
- Strolling around the grounds but not entering into the house?
- Sitting on the porch together but not going into the house?
- Taking him or her to the formal living room, where you will have coffee or a drink while sitting in separate chairs, then playing chess or Scrabble?
- Settling down in a cozy den where there's a fire going in the fireplace and you can sit and chat on the same sofa and catch up with things?
- Sharing a formal dinner, prepared in advance, in the dining room?
- Hanging out in the kitchen, preparing an informal meal,

eating it in the breakfast nook, cleaning up together, then watching a video?

- Spending the time in your library or exhibit room, sur-rounded by books, artwork, photos, or other objects that have special meaning for you, either personally or profes-sionally, and discussing them?
- Inviting other friends or family over to share any one of the above experiences?

This visualization can help loving fathers and daughters to see where they stand with each other at present, whether they are happier under formal or informal circumstances, concentrating on each other or some activity, being alone or part of a group, sharing personal interests or avoiding them. Which is the right place to be? Whichever place is most comfortable.

It's perfectly fine for loving fathers and daughters to cordon off certain parts of their lives from one another. That's what it means to be adults leading separate lives. Cordoning off areas that bring unproductive conflict allows partners to share what they can share in peace.

Cara and her father, Tony, had no trouble sharing their com-mon interest in movies, gardening, and baseball but differed strongly on security issues. Cara looked for work to be challenging and fulfilling, whereas, for Tony, the most important thing was the paycheck.

When Cara mentioned her plan to give up her fifteen-year ten-ure with a major corporation to work for a nonprofit agency, Tony tried to scare her out of it.

"If you make this move," he warned her, "you'll lose your pen-sion and medical benefits. And for what? It would be crazy. You're just going through a restless phase. You'll get over it."

But Cara, who had learned that they would never agree on such issues, merely said, "Thanks for your input, Dad. Now, do you think the Mets really have a chance this time?"

Of course, Tony was far from satisfied with this response. He was sincerely worried about Cara. But Cara had learned long ago to draw certain lines, and Tony had agreed to observe them. It wasn't an easy process, but it was worth it and leaves them free to talk about baseball, gardening, and the movies.

Healing

Even among loving fathers and daughters, there's sometimes a good deal of residual bitterness left from the shared past. Such bitterness calls for healing. Healing is a process of coming to know, accept, forgive, enjoy, and rejoice in the other as a whole and separate human being—individual and equal, at once intimate and appropriately distanced.

Healing is hastened by getting to know the reality of your father or daughter, outside of their subpersonalities and roles. We've dealt with this issue before, especially in chapter 10, "Getting Closer"; but both healing and getting closer are processes that can always be taken further.

For fathers and daughters who love each other but don't know what to talk about, here are some questions that may open up new possibilities. Obviously, you don't want to interrogate each other with many questions at a time, so what is offered here should supply material for many, many conversations.

Questions to Ask a Daughter

How is your work life going? How are you doing these days in school or at work? Do you feel you're in the right field for you? What are your career goals? What's the next step? What do you think of your boss? How do you like the people you work with? Do you think you'll stay there or move on? What's more important, your feelings about the work or how much it pays?

How is your personal life going? What's going well in your private life? What are you hoping to change? What are your personal goals? Any way I can help?

What activities do you enjoy? What books have you been reading? What movies or concerts have you been seeing? What music do you listen to? Anything you can recommend? Who are your favorite performers? What games do you play? (How about selecting a show or a concert for us to go to together? If you're a participant or a performer, when can I come to watch you?)

What are your values? Which political party do you belong to? What are your reasons? Who are the public figures you admire? Who don't you like? Which issues do you think are most important? What kind of a society would you like to live in? Are you active in any organizations? What do you think an individual can do to change things?

Questions to Ask a Father

What was it like at home when you were a kid? Were you closer to your mother or your father? What kind of things did you and your brothers and sisters do together? Were your parents affectionate or harsh? Did they play favorites and where did you fit in the family pecking order? What got you into trouble and how were you punished? What won you approval and how were you rewarded? (Have you got old pictures you could show me?)

What activities did you enjoy? Did you read much? What was your favorite book? What were your favorite radio or television shows? What were your favorite movies? What was the music you liked? Who were your favorite performers? Did you play an instrument? Did you ever play in an orchestra or a band? (What if I read the book and we talked about it? Have you got some old records I could listen to? How about renting the video of your favorite old movie so we can watch it?)

What games and sports did you like best? Did you like mental games, cards, or sports? Were you mainly a spectator or did you play, too? What position did you play? Who were your favorite players? (Shall we buy a set of your favorite game and play it together? Would you like the two of us to go to a ball game together?)

What about your life outside your home? How did you feel about school? Who are the teachers you remember? What was the worst thing that ever happened to you at school? What was the best thing? Who were your friends? Did you have a best friend? What did you do together? What ever happened to him? (Have you got trophies or yearbooks or memorabilia from your school days to show me?)

What were your teens like? Were they hard or easy? Were you popular or a loner? Who did you hang out with? Who was your first major crush? Did you date? What did you do on dates? Did you drink or take drugs? What do you believe were the effects?

How did you envision your future when you were a kid? Who were your heroes? What did you want to be when you grew up? Are you disappointed or satisfied with the way things turned out? Do you like your work? What would you rather be doing? What are you hoping to do with your life from now on?

What are your values? Which political party do you belong to, and why? Who are the public figures you admire, or don't? Which issues do you think are important? What do you think an individual can do?

The Power of Honest Answers

If you can ask and answer relatively impersonal questions like these, you may be able to move on later to more sensitive matters—such as your personal relationships, your marriages, your failures and losses, your shared past. But don't get into subjects where you would be uneasy with the truth. Mostly, when we avoid the truth with a parent or child, it's because we want to maintain an image. Images don't have faults, but images also can't grow.

In a powerfully affecting article, *Ourselves as Nonfiction*, Harry Stein says of confessing to his youthful indiscretions:

> That's what we owe our kids: *ourselves*—up close and personal, as nonfiction. Indeed, there is perhaps no greater gift we can offer than the certainty of our own fallibility, our own struggles to come to terms with the world.[11]

As father and daughter draw closer together, they can begin to play "remember when?"—fishing for those memories that unite them and excite tenderness and humor.

We have previously discussed the importance of writing letters, both angry and loving, not meant to be sent. But fathers and daughters well advanced in the healing process can write letters and send them. Here is the opening of a letter written by a client to her father during the course of their healing process:

> Dear Dad,
>   I want to thank you for taking me to the park when I was little. I remember holding your hand and walking to the park and sitting on the bench. Thank you for the jokes and laughter we would share on Christmas day when you would hand out the presents individually. Thank you for always providing for the family with a paycheck and working long hours.

Then she went on:

>   I didn't like you much, Dad, for not stopping the abuse you saw go on day in and day out in our house. Why didn't you ever get tired of watching us getting hit and abused? Why didn't you ever get some psychiatric help for Mother instead of settling for a family doctor's opinions?

Healing fathers and daughters bring up their old hurts not to dwell on them, or to make the other feel guilty, or to justify anger and alienation, but to settle the issue and leave it behind.

Role Reversal

Occasionally a daughter is called on to play parent to her father, who is virtually turned into a child through illness or old age.

In *Daddyboy*, Carol Wolfe Konek describes her father, cruelly altered by Alzheimer's Disease:

I see him standing in the hallway staring at a vision in the weave of the carpet, naked from the waist down, absurdly wearing a stocking cap, a shirt, and two jackets.[12]

In the patriarchal past, one daughter was sometimes kept at home for life, to tend her parents in their old age. Even in the early twentieth century, daughters were still expected to become their fathers' nurses, even daughters like Margaret Mitchell or Anna Freud with important careers of their own.

Today, such expectations strike us as unfair and outmoded. Yet, aging parents need care and loving children may want to take care of them. Looking after an ailing parent can be a gratifying pleasure, not merely a grim duty. For some, it's a last chance to clear up unfinished business or attempt a reconciliation. And where money is short and affordable care is not available, sometimes there's no alternative.

For those with a choice, what is the right thing to do? There is no longer an automatic answer. A truly loving father will not assume that his daughter's foremost reason for existence is to serve him.

Ronald Pulleyblank, a California electrical engineer, has Amyotrophic Lateral Sclerosis (Lou Gehrig's disease), and is almost completely paralyzed. He recently published an article on how the situation looks from the viewpoint of the loving husband of a professional woman and father of two daughters in college.

Ronald Pulleyblank very much wants to be at home with his family and has so far accepted many sacrifices to keep him there, but he has also established limits as to how much of a burden he is willing to be. As the time of this writing, his insurer was only paying for two eight-hour nursing shifts a day and he needed three. The family savings which had paid for the third shift were now depleted. He was suing the insurer, but if he lost, either his family would have to take over the nursing chores, or Ronald would have to go into the hospital.

This is what Ronald Pulleyblank decided:

At this point, I want to live, even on life support, even if I can't live at home.

This is my illness. Others should not be made miserable so that I can be happy.

Consequently, I have decided that:

My children will not be in my home, with responsibility for the operation of my life-sustaining equipment.

My wife will not give up her private practice as a psychotherapist specializing in family therapy to become my nurse for eight hours a day.

Therefore, if we lose my 24-hour nursing care, we have decided that, in order to live, I will have to return to the hospital.

Caught between disease, financial crisis and legal battles with giant institutions, we have lost much of the control we once had over our lives. But, in the midst of it all, life still brings us satisfaction and pleasures. We hope for the best.[13]

This sounds like the choice of a loving father. But it is not the only one possible. He might have chosen to go into the hospital before the savings were used up. He might have let his family carry one shift a day. He might have asked his daughters to alternate in taking one year off from college so he could stay home for two more years. He might have ended his life sometime in the past by going off life support.

Any of these choices would have been defensible. What matters is that he never assumed that, because they were female, his wife and daughters should permanently sacrifice their happiness to his. In that, he was a true *contemporary* loving father.

Transcendence

When an aging father dies, his daughter is at once set free and abandoned. The father is no longer there to supervise, control, help, advise, dominate, support, criticize, and love. If it hasn't been done before, there's no reason not to make peace with him now.

The father's death is his final letting go, his final surrender of control. But if the relationship has been loving, the preparation has gone on from the start. The first time the baby daughter is allowed to toddle off into the next room alone; the first time she is sent out to play in the yard with no one to watch; the first time she crosses the street without her hand being held; the first day she goes to school: all these little separations are foreshadowings of the final one.

The greatest foreshadowing of all comes when the child goes out into the world. In an essay, "Honoring a Daughter's Emergence into Womanhood," Tom Pinkson describes both the pain and the astonished discovery:

> My eighteen-year-old daughter left home today. She walked out the door and broke my heart. Somehow it seems so unfair that after all this time and effort of raising, nurturing, and caring for her, she just up and leaves. . . . I feel grief and sadness, my heart torn open . . .
>
> I think back to what my parents must have gone through when I left home at seventeen. Then, I didn't have any awareness about what feelings were stirred in them by my leaving. I was totally caught up in my adolescent self-absorption and the adventure that lay before me. Now I feel what I imagine was their pain along with my own. I feel very joined with them.

Tom's awareness of repeating his parents' experience was a revelation. By letting go of his daughter, he gained a greater understanding of his parents and of the flow of life. By relinquishing control, he gained wisdom and peace. The love he had thought he had lost was returned to him in another form.

Carol Wolfe Konek celebrated the peace she felt upon letting go of her Alzheimer-ruined father:

> As my father left his fragile body, as he vanished behind a veil of confusion and silence, he became more vivid, more vibrant, in my mind's eye. I am startled by the realization that I am

Leonard's daughter, dining with Linus Pauling, and that, although Leonard cannot know this, there is a circle completing itself in the double moment of knowing myself as discrete and connected. I embody his legacy of reverence for peace and respect for science.[15]

Well after her father's death, the silent-film star Gloria Swanson made peace with what had clearly been a difficult relationship:

No two people can ever get to know each other completely. My father's life had been his to live. He had made all his own choices. I had no right, as another person, even as his only daughter, to question the choices he had made, just as I felt no one had any right ultimately to question my choices regarding my own life.[16]

Fathers and daughters can both receive this gift of transcendence, but only on condition that they have made peace with the past and with life. In a state of transcendence, we take the good we have received and gladly forget the rest. And, in doing so, we know that nothing good is ever lost.

Novelist George Eliot (Mary Ann Evans) put it best:

Oh, the comfort, the inexpressible comfort, of feeling safe with a person, having neither to weigh thoughts nor measure words, but to pour them all out, just as it is, chaff and grain together, knowing that a faithful friend will take and sift them, keeping what is worth keeping, and then, with the breath of kindness, blowing the rest away.[17]

NOTES

Chapter One: Invitation to the Dance

1. The autobiographical books referred to are Germaine Greer's *Daddy, We Hardly Knew You* (New York: Knopf, 1990); Kate Millett's *The Loony Bin Trap* (New York: Simon & Schuster, 1990); and Gloria Steinem's *Revolution from Within* (New York: Little, Brown, 1992). The novels are Gail Godwin's *Father Melancholy's Daughter* (New York: William Morrow, 1991) and Mona Simpson's *The Lost Father* (New York: Knopf, 1992).

2. The Men's Movement books referred to are Robert Bly's *Iron John* (Reading, Mass.: Addison-Wesley, 1990) and Sam Keen's *Fire in the Belly* (New York: Bantam, 1991). John Bradshaw's books are too numerous to list, and his PBS television series *On the Family* has reached millions.

3. Quoted in "Ice Cube's Rap On How to Avoid Ghetto Meltdown," *San Francisco Examiner Datebook*, 14 July 1991, 35.

4. Louis Sullivan's report was summarized and excerpted in the *San Francisco Examiner* on January 10, 1992. A number of corroborating reports were released in January of 1992. These include a Centers for Disease Control study showing that in 1988 over a million babies were born to unmarried women, the most ever; this figure represented 26 percent of U.S. births, compared to 18 percent in 1980, and a five-fold increase since 1960. Among blacks, the percentage was 63 percent. Of households with children, 19.4 were headed by single mothers, while only 2.1 percent were headed by single fathers. A study by Victor Fuchs and Diana Reklis of Stanford University, published in the January 1992 edition of *Science,* indicates that today's children are less well off mentally and physically than children of thirty years ago. Their standardized test scores in school are fifty points lower, and they are three times more likely to commit suicide or be murdered. According to Fuchs and Reklis, families with an adult male present spent an average of $7,640 per child in 1988,

whereas those without a father present had only $2,397 to spend. The growing prevalence of abandonment is attested to by statistics. In a news article entitled "It's the Kids Who Pay If the Dads Don't" (*San Francisco Examiner*, 29 September 1991, A1), Carol Ness summarizes the painful figures: 1.3 million active cases of financial abandonment by fathers in California alone, up 50 percent in five years.

5. The speculations of Belsky, Steinberg, Macoby, and others were reported on pages B5 and B6 of the *New York Times* on 29 July 1991, in an article entitled "Theory Links Early Puberty to Childhood Stress," by Daniel Goleman. Some researchers stress biological changes: a 1990 study by Dr. Michele Surbey of the University of Toronto followed 1,123 girls whose parents divorced and found that they began their periods an average of four months earlier than girls from intact families. A study by Dr. Charles Snowden, a psychiatrist at the University of Wisconsin, found that young monkeys who were separated from their parents also had an earlier onset of puberty. Some researchers, however, such as Dr. Macoby, stress environmental factors, noting that children from broken homes receive less supervision.

6. Margo Maine, *Father Hunger: Fathers, Daughters and Food* (Carlsbad, Calif.: Gurze Books, 1991).

7. The matrilocal systems of Southeast Asia and the Pacific are not controversial, having been noted both by early explorers and modern anthropologists. In *The Origin of the Japanese Language* (Tokyo: Kokusai Bunka Shinkokai, 1970) author Ohno Susumu takes for granted their penetration into West Japan and their partial survival into the Heian period (800–1100). Powerful corroboration exists in Heian literature, especially in *The Tale of Genji*, which dramatizes such customs as young couples living with the bride's parents, women inheriting the family property, daughters preferred over sons, and female priests, shamans, and scholars, etc.

8. Aeschylus, *The Furies (Eumenides)* Verses 605–608. (B. Goulter supplied the translation.)

9. According to an article, "Battered Women: Why Do They Stay?" in the News and Trends section of *Psychology Today* (May/June 1992), in 70 percent of custody cases *in which the father has been accused of child battery*, the father accused of the abuse gets custody of the child. Phyllis Chesler discusses the subject in depth in *Mothers on Trial: The Battle for Children and Custody* (New York: Harcourt Brace Jovanovich, 1985).

10. The Ona story is from R. Briffault, *The Mothers*, 3 vols. (New York: Macmillan, 1927), 1: 342; 2: 545; discussed by Wolfgang Lederer in *The Fear of Women* (New York: a Harvest Book, Harcourt Brace Jovanovich, 1968), 151–52.

11. Dr. Benjamin's paper, "Like Subjects and Love Objects," was presented to the American Psychoanalytic Association Symposium in San Francisco in March 1992.

12. Ibid.

13. Ibid.

14. Dr. Renik's paper, "Men and Women Love in the Same Way—Only Differently," was presented to the American Psychoanalytic Association Symposium in San Francisco, in March 1992.

15. Ruth McClendon and Leslie B. Kadis, *Chocolate Pudding and Other Approaches to Intensive Multiple-Family Therapy* (Palo Alto: Science and Behavior Books, 1983), 306.

Chapter Two: The Lost Father and His Yearning Daughter

1. "The Uncensored Paglia," *IMAGE*, Sunday, July 7, 1991, 10.

2. The material on Marilyn Monroe was garnered from many published sources. Barney Ruditsky was a friend of Barbara Goulter's family and a relative by marriage; he personally spoke of the wrong-door incident and of Monroe's hiring detectives to search for her father.

3. The O'Neill, Vanderbilt, and Marcus stories were garnered from many sources, but we are especially indebted to Gloria Vanderbilt's *Black Knight, White Knight* (New York: Knopf, 1987) and Aram Saroyan's *Trio, Portrait of an Intimate Friendship* (New York: Simon & Schuster, 1985 and New York: Penguin, 1986). Aram Saroyan is Carol Marcus's son.

4. The stories of Chaplin waiting while Oona shopped and her attempts to make her bedroom like a tomb are recounted in *Trio*.

5. According to the obituary of Oona Chaplin in the *San Francisco Examiner* of September 28, 1991, she was a "recluse since her husband's death in 1977," seldom appearing in public and not even attending the celebration of the one-hundredth anniversary of Chaplin's birth. When his coffin was stolen and held for ransom, she refused to pay, saying that he was not in his coffin but "in heaven and in my heart." She was survived by her eight children and seventeen grandchildren.

6. Vanderbilt, 201.

7. Ibid., 136.

8. Ibid., 201.

9. Ibid., 246.
10. Arthur Waley, *The No Plays of Japan* (New York: Grove Press, 1957). "Kagekiyo" by Seami appears on pages 123–33. The quotations throughout the next several pages are sequential.
11. Deborah Tannen, Ph.D., made these observations in a PBS special on communication between the sexes, broadcast on KQED, San Francisco, in March 1992. Related ideas are developed in her *You Just Don't Understand: Women and Men in Conversation* (New York: Ballantine, 1990).
12. This unpublished paper, "The Inability to Achieve Mutual Love," was presented by Dr. Person at the American Psychoanalytic Association Symposium, San Francisco, March 1992.
13. Dana Crawley Jack, *Silencing the Self: Women and Depression* (Cambridge: Harvard University Press, 1992).

Chapter Three: The Abusive Father and His Victim Daughter

1. Entry of June 16, 1847. From *The Private Diary of Leo Tolstoy 1853–57*, ed. Aylmer Maude (London, 1927). Quoted by Paul Johnson in *Intellectuals* (New York: Harper and Row, 1988).
2. Stephen Karpman, "Script Drama Analysis," *Transactional Analysis Bulletin* 7:26, Berkeley, Calif. April 1968.
3. Some of the mutilations inflicted upon women are so cruel as to seem unbelievable, yet they have been documented beyond a doubt. For details on foot binding, we recommend Howard S. Levy, *Chinese Footbinding: The History of a Curious Erotic Custom* (New York: Walton Rawls, 1966). Among numerous recent studies of female "circumcision" are Fran Hosken, *The Hosken Report: Genital and Sexual Mutilation of Females* (Lexington, Mass.: Women's International Network News, 1979); M. B. Assad, "Female Circumcision in Egypt: Current Research and Social Implications," *Seminar on Traditional Practices Affecting the Health of Women and Children* (Alexandria, Egypt WHO/ EMRO Technical Publications, 1980); Lilian Passmore Sanderson, *Against the Mutilation of Women* (London: Ithaca Press, 1981); and Hanny Lightfoot-Klein, *Prisoners of Ritual: An Odyssey into Female Genital Circumcision in Africa* (New York: Harrington Park Press, 1989). The prevalence of the custom in Africa is also the subject of Alice Walker's novel *Possessing the Secret of Joy* (Orlando, Fla.: Harcourt Brace Jovanovich, 1992). Marilyn French provides an overview of both foot binding (99) and female genital mutilation in *The War Against Women* (New York: Summit Books, 1992) (106–14). French

also documents the use of clitoridectomy in the United States and Europe during the nineteenth century and as late as the 1930s as a "cure" for masturbation and "nymphomania" (110–11). Jeffrey Moussaieff Masson provides extensive confirmation in *The Dark Science: Women, Sexuality and Psychiatry in the Nineteenth Century* (New York: Farrar, Straus & Giroux, 1986). And let's not forget that the severe corseting of Victorian women, which caused them to faint at the slightest exertion, along with the crippling of women's feet by high-heeled shoes and their systematic starvation through socially approved dieting are but milder forms of the same tendency to mutilate females in the name of entirely artificial standards of beauty and/or attempts to render them feeble and helpless.

Chapter Four: The Pampering Father and His Spoiled Daughter

1. Warren Beatty's remark (from a television interview with David Frost) is quoted by Aaron Latham, in "Fathering the Nest, The New American Manhood," *M*, May 1992, 69.

2. Material on Jacqueline Kennedy Onassis has been gleaned from numerous published sources, primarily from Peter Collier and David Horowitz, *The Kennedys* (New York: Warner, 1985).

3. *The Tale of Genji* exists in two English translations, one by Arthur Waley (New York: Modern Library, 1960) and the other by Edward Seidensticker (New York: Knopf, 1976). It is the earliest known novel from any culture that concerns itself with dramatizing domestic life and probing the complex motives of its characters. The society described on the following pages is based largely on *The Tale of Genji*, Murasaki's diary, and the journals of other women writers of the period, such as *The Pillowbook of Sei Shonagon*, trans. Ivan Morris (New York: Columbia University Press, 1967) and *The Confessions of Lady Nijo*, trans. Karen Brazell (Garden City: N.Y.: Anchor Press/Doubleday, 1973).

Chapter Five: The Pygmalion Father and His Companion Daughter

1. The events of Shirley Abbott's life are gleaned from her two autobiographical books, *Womenfolks: Growing Up Down South* (New York: Ticknor & Fields, 1983) and *The Bookmaker's Daughter* (New York: Ticknor & Fields, 1991) plus Elizabeth Devereaux's interview with the author in *Publishers Weekly*, 5 July 1991, 48–49.

2. Among sources for information on Anna Freud are: Lucy Freeman and Dr. Herbert S. Stream, *Freud and Women* (New York: The Con-

tinuum Publishing Corp., 1987); Robert Coles, *Anna Freud, The Dream of Psychoanalysis* (Reading, Mass.: Addison-Wesley, 1991); Peter Gay, *Freud: A Life for Our Time* (New York: Norton, 1988).

3. On May 13, 1938, little over a year before his death, at a time when he was being cared for by Anna almost full-time, Freud referred in a letter to his son Ernst to the supposedly innate "physiological feeble-mindedness of women" and their "dislike for thinking altogether." (Quoted in Freeman and Stream, *Freud and Women.*) It is to be noted that at this date his daughter Anna was world famous as an analyst and theorist and had been his self-sacrificing "Antigone" for many years. Quoted in Freeman and Stream.

4. The dynamic among Tolstoy, his wife, Sonia, and his daughter Sasha is a central theme of Anne Edwards's *Sonya: The Life of Countess Tolstoy* (London: Carroll & Graf, 1981). Also useful is Paul Johnson's "Tolstoy: God's Elder Brother," in *Intellectuals* (New York: Harper & Row, 1988) 107–37.

5. Johnson, 121.

6. Results summarized in Laura Myers, "Study Finds Women Pay Dearly for Career Gaps," *San Francisco Examiner,* 10 January 1992, A1.

7. Signe Hammer, *Passionate Attachments: Fathers and Daughters in America Today* (New York: Rawson, 1982), 173–87.

8. Ibid., 179.

9. Ibid.

Chapter Six: The Ruined Father and His Rescuing Daughter

1. Marilyn French, *Shakespeare's Division of Experience* (New York: Summit, 1981), 27.

2. Greer, *Daddy, We Hardly Knew You,* 3.

3. Information on Margaret Mitchell was gleaned primarily from Ann Edwards, *The Road to Tara: The Life of Margaret Mitchell* (New York: Dell, 1991); Elizabeth I. Hanson, *Margaret Mitchell* (Boston: Dwayne, 1991); and, above all, from Darden Asbury Pyron, *Southern Daughter: The Life of Margaret Mitchell* (New York: Oxford University Press, 1991).

4. Maybelle's deathbed letter to Margaret appears in Pyron, 91.

5. Pyron, 403–4.

6. Judy Cameron and Paul J. Christian, *The Art of Gone with the Wind* (New York: Prentice-Hall Press, 1989), 230.

7. Desmond Morris, *Manwatching: A Field Guide to Human Behavior* (New York: Harry N. Abrams, 1977), 256–7.

8. This phenomenon was described by Lloyd G. Humphreys in "Reinforcement as a Variable Ratio," in *Readings in Learning* (New York: Prentice-Hall, 1953). We believe that it deserves more attention than it has received.

Chapter Seven: The Anguished Father and His Angry Daughter

1. References to Colburn from Mark St. John Erickson, "The Anger That Stirs Within," *San Francisco Examiner*, 2 May 1992, D1.
2. Ibid.
3. Albert Ellis, Ph.D., and Robert A. Harper, Ph.D., *A New Guide to Rational Living* (North Hollywood: Melvin Powers, Wilshire Book Company, 1979), 116.
4. Biographical materials on Sylvia Plath have been gleaned from numerous published sources, most notably Linda Wagner-Martin's *Sylvia Plath, A Biography* (New York: Simon & Schuster, 1987) and *Ariel Ascending, Writings on Sylvia Plath*, ed. Paul Alexander (New York: Harper & Row, 1985).
5. Sylvia Plath, "Daddy," in *Ariel* (New York: Harper & Row, 1965), 49–51.
6. Elizabeth Hardwick, "Sylvia Plath," in *Seduction and Betrayal: Women and Literature* (New York: Random House, 1970), 107. "Sylvia Plath" was also reprinted in Alexander.

Chapter Eight: The Dance of the Mother-Raised Children

1. Dorothy Dinnerstein, *The Mermaid and the Minotaur: Sexual Arrangements and the Human Malaise* (New York: Harper Colophon, 1977), 12.
2. Dinnerstein, 115–56.
3. Jeff Miller, "The First Language," *UCSF Magazine*, February 1992, 30–35, reports on Sandra Weiss's findings.
4. Ibid., 33.
5. Ibid., 34.
6. Brazelton's findings are summarized in Barbara Meltz, "Touching Tribute to Children," *San Francisco Examiner*, 23 May 1992, D1.
7. Tiffany Field's and Ed Tronick's work is also discussed by Meltz.
8. The Barnet study is summarized in Aaron Latham, "Dad Again," *M*, May 1992, 71–75.
9. Arlie Hochschild, *The Second Shift: Working Parents and the Revolution at Home* (New York: Viking Penguin, 1989).
10. Lillian Smith, *Killers of the Dream* (New York: Norton, 1961), 28–29.

11. Richard Louv, *Childhood's Future* (Boston: Houghton Mifflin Company, 1990), 72–73.
12. Ibid.
13. Carol Gilligan *In a Different Voice: Psychological Theory and Human Development* (Cambridge: Harvard University Press, 1982).
14. Gilligan, 24–39. Kohlberg studies moral development in children, defining a series of stages which Gilligan indicates are based on a strictly male model. He is the author of *The Philosophy of Moral Development* (San Francisco: Harper & Row, 1981). The dilemma discussed by Gilligan is one devised by Kohlberg.
15. The study that Gilligan describes is Susan Pollak and Carol Gilligan, "Images of Violence in Thematic Apperception Test Stories," *Journal of Personality and Social Psychology* 42, no 1 (1982): 159–67.

Chapter Nine: Solo Dances

1. Lewis B. Smedes, *Forgive and Forget: Healing the Hurts We Don't Deserve* (San Francisco: Harper & Row, 1984), 73.
2. Simpson, *The Lost Father*, 451.
3. Ibid., 475.
4. Ibid., 503–4.
5. Mary McClure Goulding and Robert L. Goulding, *Changing Lives through Redecision Therapy* (New York: Brunner/Mazel, 1979).
6. Carol Tavris, *The Mismeasure of Woman* (New York: Simon & Schuster, 1992).
7. Harville Hendrix, Ph.D., *Getting the Love You Want: A Guide for Couples* (New York: Henry Holt, 1988) and *Keeping the Love You Find: A Guide for Singles* (New York: Pocket, 1992). Our commentary is based on the general substance of his ideas rather than specific passages. The lecture referred to took place in San Francisco, on June 12, 1992.
8. Smedes, 72.

Chapter Ten: Getting Closer

1. M. Scott Peck, *The Different Drum: Community Making and Peace* (New York: Touchstone, Simon & Schuster, 1987).
2. Victor Goertzel and Mildred George Goertzel, *Cradles of Eminence* (Boston: Little, Brown, 1962).
3. Ibid., 75–77. The Goertzels' profile of Eleanor Roosevelt draws upon published biographical materials.
4. The Goertzels find so many cases of children succeeding brilliantly in fields where their parents have failed and attributing their success to

their parents that they consider it a characteristic trait of the eminent.

Chapter Eleven: Loving Father and Loving Daughter

1. George F. Simons, *Keeping Your Personal Journal* (New York: Ballantine 1978), 3.
2. The quotation from Fanny Mendelssohn is from the Bay Area Women's Philharmonic Announcement, spring 1992.
3. Bob Greene, *Good Morning, Merry Sunshine* (New York: Penguin, 1985), 238.
4. Jack Kornfield, "Parenting as Spiritual Practice," in *Fathers, Sons, and Daughters,* ed. Charles Scull, Ph.D. (Los Angeles: Jeremy P. Tarcher, 1992), 38.
5. Eleanor Roosevelt's tribute to her father is from *The Autobiography of Eleanor Roosevelt* and is quoted in L. Norma Cox, ed. *Dear Dad: Famous People's Loving Letters to Their Fathers* (New York: Saybook, 1987).
6. Leatrice Gilbert Fountain's comment on John Gilbert is also collected in Cox.
7. Uta Hagen's letter is also in Cox.
8. The anecdotes about Clinton and his daughter were reported in the *New York Times,* 15 July 1992, A12.
9. Carol Wolfe Konek, *Daddyboy: A Memoir* (St. Paul: Graywolf Press, 1991), 100–101.
10. Brumberg's study is reported in "Dear Diary," *Psychology Today,* May/June 1992, News and Trends section. Quotations are taken from the account.
11. Harry Stein, "Ourselves as Nonfiction," *Psychology Today,* May/June 1992, 24–26, 77.
12. Konek, 120.
13. Ronald Pulleyblank, "My Symptom Is Stillness," *The Family Therapy Networker,* March/April 1992, 62–70.
14. Tom Pinkson, "Honoring a Daughter's Emergence into Womanhood," in Scull, ed.
15. Konek, 158.
16. Gloria Swanson, *Swanson on Swanson* (New York: Random House, 1980), 200.
17. The George Eliot quotation can be found in Alice and Walden Howard, *Exploring the Road Less Traveled* (New York: Simon & Schuster, 1985), 41.

BIBLIOGRAPHY

Abbott, Shirley. *The Bookmaker's Daughter.* New York: Ticknor & Fields, 1991.

———. Interview by Elizabeth Devereaux in *Publishers Weekly,* 5 July 1991, 48–49.

———. *Womenfolks: Growing Up Down South.* New York: Ticknor & Fields, 1983.

Aeschylus. *Eumenides* (The Furies). Translated by Richard Lattimore. Chicago: University of Chicago Press, 1969.

Alexander, Paul, ed. *Ariel Ascending, Writings on Sylvia Plath.* New York: Harper & Row, 1985.

Assad, M. B. "Female Circumcision in Egypt: Current Research and Social Implications." *Seminar on Traditional Practices Affecting the Health of Women and Children.* Alexandria, Egypt: WHO/EMRO Technical Publications, 1980.

"Battered Women: Why Do They Stay?" *Psychology Today,* May/June, 1992, News and Trends section.

Benjamin, Jessica, Ph.D. "Like Subjects and Love Objects: A Perspective on Gender Development and Identificatory Love." Paper presented at the American Psychoanalytic Association Symposium, San Francisco, March 1992.

Bly, Robert. *Iron John.* Reading, Mass.: Addison-Wesley, 1990.

Briffault, R. *The Mothers.* 3 vols. New York: Macmillan, 1927.

Chesler, Phyllis. *Mothers on Trial: The Battle for Children and Custody.* New York: Harcourt Brace Jovanovich, 1985.

Chodorow, Nancy. *The Reproduction of Mothering: Psychoanalysis and the Sociology of Gender.* Berkeley: University of California Press, 1978.

Coles, Robert. *Anna Freud, The Dream of Psychoanalysis.* Reading, Mass.: Addison-Wesley, 1991.

Collier, Peter, and David Horowitz. *The Kennedys.* New York: Warner, 1985.

Cox, L. Norma. *Dear Dad: Famous People's Loving Letters to Their Fathers.* New York: Saybrook, 1987.

"Dear Diary." *Psychology Today,* May/June 1992, 18.

Devereaux, Elizabeth. "Interview with Shirley Abbott." Publishers Weekly, 5 July 1991, 48–49.

Dinnerstein, Dorothy. *The Mermaid and the Minotaur: Sexual Arrangements and the Human Malaise.* New York: Harper Colophon, 1977.

Edwards, Anne. *The Road to Tara: The Life of Margaret Mitchell.* New York: Dell, 1991.

———.*Sonya: The Life of Countess Tolstoy.* London: Carroll & Graf, 1981.

Ellis, Albert, Ph.D., and Robert A. Harper, Ph.D. *A New Guide to Rational Living.* North Hollywood: Melvin Powers, Wilshire Book Company, 1979.

Erickson, Mark St. John. "The Anger that Stirs Within." *San Francisco Examiner,* 2 May 1992, D1.

Fountain, Leatrice Gilbert. *Dark Star: The Untold Story of the Meteoric Rise and Fall of the Legendary John Gilbert.* New York: St. Martin's, 1985.

Freeman, Lucy, and Dr. Herbert S. Stream. *Freud and Women.* New York: The Continuum Publishing Company, 1987.

French, Marilyn. *Shakespeare's Division of Experience.* New York: Summit, 1981.

———. *The War Against Women.* New York: Summit, 1992.

Gay, Peter. *Freud: A Life for Our Time.* New York: Norton, 1988.

Gilligan, Carol. *In a Different Voice: Psychological Theory and Human Development.* Cambridge: Harvard University Press, 1982.

———, and Susan Pollak. "Images of Violence in Thematic Apperception Test Stories." *Journal of Personality and Social Psychology* 42, no 1 (1982): 159–67.

Godwin, Gail. *Father Melancholy's Daughter.* New York: Morrow, 1991.

Goertzel, Victor, and Mildred George. *Cradles of Eminence.* Boston: Little, Brown, 1962.

Goleman, Daniel. "Theory Links Early Puberty to Childhood Stress." *New York Times,* 29 July 1991, B5–B6.

Goulding, Mary McClure, and Robert L. Goulding. *Changing Lives Through Redecision Therapy.* New York: Brunner/Mazel, 1979.

Greene, Bob. *Good Morning, Merry Sunshine.* New York: Penguin, 1985.

Greer, Germaine. *Daddy, We Hardly Knew You.* New York: Knopf, 1990.

———. *The Female Eunuch.* New York: McGraw-Hill, 1971.

Hagen, Uta. Quoted in Cox.

Hammer, Signe. *Passionate Attachments: Fathers and Daughters in America Today.* New York: Rawson, 1982.

Hammerstein, Oscar, and Richard Rodgers. "Soliloquy," from *Carousel.* New York: Williamson Music, 1945.

238

Hanson, Elizabeth I. *Margaret Mitchell.* Boston: Dwayne, 1991.

Hardwick, Elizabeth. "Sylvia Plath." In *Seduction and Betrayal: Women and Literature.* New York: Random House, 1970.

Hendrix, Harville, Ph.D. *Getting the Love You Want: A Guide for Couples.* New York: Henry Holt, 1988.

———. *Keeping the Love You Find: A Guide for Singles.* New York: Pocket, 1992.

Hochschild, Arlie. *The Second Shift: Working Parents and the Revolution at Home.* New York: Viking Penguin, 1989.

Hosken, Fran. *The Hosken Report: Genital and Sexual Mutilation of Females.* Lexington, Mass.: Women's International Network News, 1979.

Howard, Alice, and Walden. *Exploring the Road Less Traveled.* New York: Simon & Schuster, 1985.

Humphreys, Lloyd G. "Reinforcement at a Variable Ratio." In *Readings in Learning.* New York: Prentice-Hall, 1953.

"Ice Cube's Rap On How to Avoid Ghetto Meltdown." *San Francisco Chronicle-Examiner Datebook,* 14 July 1991, 35.

Jack, Dana Crawley. *Silencing the Self: Women and Depression.* Cambridge: Harvard University Press, 1992.

Johnson, Paul. "Tolstoy: God's Elder Brother." In *Intellectuals.* New York: Harper & Row, 1988.

Kadis, Leslie B., and Ruth McClendon. *Chocolate Pudding and Other Approaches to Intensive Multiple-Family Therapy.* Palo Alto: Science and Behavior Books, 1983.

"Kagekiyo," by Seami. See Waley, Arthur. *The No Plays of Japan.* New York: Grove Press, 1957, 123–33.

Karpman, Stephen. "Script Drama Analysis." *Transactional Analysis Bulletin* 7:26, Berkeley, Calif., April 1968.

Keen, Sam. *Fire in the Belly.* New York: Bantam, 1991.

Kohlberg, Lawrence. *The Philosophy of Moral Development.* San Francisco: Harper & Row, 1981.

Konek, Carol Wolfe. *Daddyboy: A Memoir.* St. Paul: Graywolf Press, 1991.

Kornfield, Jack. "Parenting as Spiritual Practice." In *Fathers, Sons, & Daughters,* edited by Charles Scull, Ph.D. Los Angeles: Jeremy P. Tarcher, Inc., 1992.

Latham, Aaron. "Dad Again." *M,* May 1992, 71–75.

———. "Fathering the Nest, The New American Manhood." *M,* May 1992, 69.

Lederer, Wolfgang. *The Fear of Women*. New York: A Harvest Book, Harcourt Brace Jovanovich, 1968.

Levine, Judith. *My Enemy, My Love: Man-Hating and Ambivalence in Women's Lives*. New York: Doubleday, 1992.

Levy, Howard S. *Chinese Footbinding: The History of a Curious Erotic Custom*. New York: Walton Rawls, 1966.

Lightfoot-Klein, Hanny. *Prisoners of Ritual: An Odyssey into Female Genital Circumcision in Africa*. New York: Harrington Park Press, 1989.

Louv, Richard. *Childhood's Future*. Boston: Houghton Mifflin, 1990.

Maine, Margo. *Father Hunger: Fathers, Daughters and Food*. Carlsbad, Calif.: Gurze Books, 1991.

Masson, Jeffrey Moussaieff. *The Dark Science: Women, Sexuality and Psychiatry in the Nineteenth Century*. New York: Farrar, Straus & Giroux, 1986.

Meltz, Barbara. "Touching Tribute to Children." *San Francisco Examiner*, 23 May 1992, D1.

Miller, Jeff. "The First Language." *UCSF Magazine*, February 1992, 30–35.

Millett, Kate. *The Loony Bin Trap*. New York: Simon & Schuster, 1990.

———. *Sexual Politics*. Garden City, N.Y.: Doubleday, 1970.

Morris, Desmond. *Manwatching: A Field Guide to Human Behavior*. New York: Harry N. Abrams, 1977.

Murasaki. See *Genji, The Tale of*.

Myers, Laura. "Study Finds Women Pay Dearly for Career Gaps." *San Francisco Examiner*, 10 January 1992, A1.

Ness, Carol. "It's the Kids Who Pay If the Dads Don't." *San Francisco Examiner*, 29 September 1991, A1.

Nijo. *The Confessions of Lady Nijo*. Translated by Karen Brazell. Garden City, N.Y.: Anchor Press/Doubleday, 1973.

Ohno, Susumu. *The Origin of the Japanese Language*. Tokyo: Kokusai Bunka Shinokokai, 1970.

"Oona Chaplin, Charles' Widow," *San Francisco Examiner*, 28 September 1991.

Renik, Owen, M.D. "Clinical Presentation: Men and Women Love in the Same Way, Only Differently." Paper presented at the American Psychoanalytic Association Symposium, San Francisco, March 1992.

Paglia, Camille. "The Uncensored Paglia." *Image*, Sunday, July 7, 1991, 10.

Peck, M. Scott. *The Different Drum: Community Making and Peace*. New York: Touchstone, Simon & Schuster, 1987.

Person, Ethel Spector, M.D. "The Inability to Achieve Mutual Love." Paper presented at the American Psychoanalytic Association Symposium, San Francisco, March 1992.

Pinkson, Tom. "Honoring a Daughter's Emergence into Womanhood." In *Fathers, Sons, and Daughters.* Edited by Charles Scull, Ph.D. Los Angeles: Jeremy P. Tarcher, 1992.

Plath, Sylvia. *Ariel.* New York: Harper & Row, 1965.

Pulleyblank, Ronald. "My Symptom is Stillness." *The Family Therapy Networker,* March/April 1992, 62–70.

Pyron, Darden Asbury. *Southern Daughter: The Life of Margaret Mitchell.* New York: Oxford University Press, 1991.

Rodgers, Richard, and Oscar Hammerstein. "Soliloquy," from *Carousel.* New York: Williamson Music Company, 1945. Copyright renewed.

Roosevelt, Eleanor. *The Autobiography of Eleanor Roosevelt.* New York: Curtis Publishing Company, 1937.

Rubin, Lillian B. *Intimate Strangers.* New York: Harper & Row, 1983.

Sanderson, Lilian Passmore. *Against the Mutilation of Women.* London: Ithaca Press, 1981.

Saroyan, Aram. *Trio, Portrait of an Intimate Friendship.* New York: Simon & Schuster, 1985 and New York: Penguin, 1986.

Seidensticker, Edward, tr. *The Tale of Genji.* New York, Knopf, 1976.

Sei Shonagon. *The Pillowbook of Sei Shonagon.* Translated by Ivan Morris. New York: Columbia University Press, 1967.

Simons, George F. *Keeping Your Personal Journal.* New York: Ballantine Books, 1978.

Simpson, Mona. *The Lost Father.* New York: Knopf, 1992.

Smedes, Lewis B. *Forgive and Forget: Healing the Hurts We Don't Deserve.* San Francisco: Harper & Row, 1984.

Smith, Lillian. *Killers of the Dream.* New York: Norton, 1961.

Stein, Harry. "Ourselves as Nonfiction." *Psychology Today,* May/June 1992, 24–26.

Steinem, Gloria. *Revolution from Within: A Book of Self-Esteem.* New York: Little, Brown, 1992.

Swanson, Gloria. *Swanson on Swanson.* New York: Random House, 1980.

Tannen, Deborah, Ph.D. *You Just Don't Understand: Women and Men in Conversation.* New York: Ballantine, 1990.

Tavris, Carol. *The Mismeasure of Woman.* New York: Simon & Schuster, 1992.

Tolstoy, Count Leo. *The Private Diary of Leo Tolstoy 1853–57.* Edited by Aylmer Maude. London: 1927.

Vanderbilt, Gloria. *Black Knight, White Knight.* New York: Knopf, 1987.

Wagner-Martin, Linda. *Sylvia Plath, A Biography.* New York: Simon & Schuster, 1987.

Waley, Arthur. *The No Plays of Japan.* New York: Grove Press, 1957.

————. *The Tale of Genji.* New York: Modern Library, 1960.

Walker, Alice. *Possessing the Secret of Joy.* Harcourt Brace Jovanovich, 1992.

243

INDEX

245